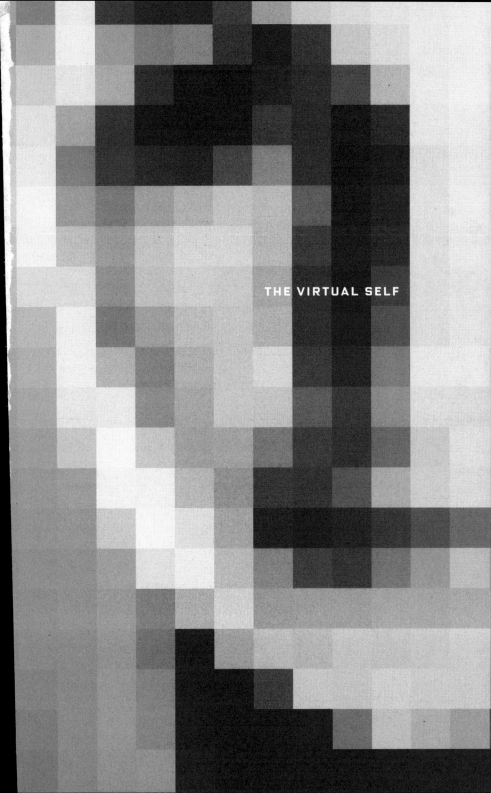

THE VIRTUAL SELF

NORA YOUNG

# THE VIRTUAL SELF

HOW OUR DIGITAL LIVES

ARE ALTERING THE WORLD

AROUND US

McClelland & Stewart

LIBRARY AND ARCHIVES CANADA CATALOGUING IN PUBLICATION

Young, Nora
The virtual self : how our digital lives are altering the world around us / Nora Young.

ISBN 978-0-7710-7064-8

1. Online social networks. 2. Social media. 3. Personal information management. I. Title.

HM851.Y68 2011      303.48'33      C2011-902128-5

We acknowledge the financial support of the Government of Canada through the Canada Book Fund and that of the Government of Ontario through the Ontario Media Development Corporation's Ontario Book Initiative. We further acknowledge the support of the Canada Council for the Arts and the Ontario Arts Council for our publishing program.

Typeset in Quadraat by M&S, Toronto

Printed and bound in Canada

ANCIENT FOREST
FRIENDLY

This book is printed on acid-free paper that is 100% recycled, ancient-forest friendly (100% post-consumer waste).

McClelland & Stewart Ltd.
75 Sherbourne Street
Toronto, Ontario
M5A 2P9
www.mcclelland.com

1 2 3 4 5      16 15 14 13 12

For my parents, Michael and Verda Young

# [ CONTENTS ]

THE VIRTUAL SELF

It was the pedometers that gave me the most trouble. I say pedometers, plural, because, in the year that I began tracking how far I walked, I went through three of them – I lost two, and a third one just stopped working. I'd forget to attach the pedometer du jour to my belt, or find that I had inadvertently hit the reset button and had erased the memory for the day. There was a period where I didn't have a pedometer at all, which threw my stats off entirely, as though I'd suddenly stopped walking and had taken to being carried by sedan chair.

I did try to monitor my movements over a period of months, but I don't think I'm naturally inclined to keep track of my behaviours, to record my exercise, my habits, and my state of mind. I'm just not very detail-oriented. I'm prone to sudden enthusiasms, and less inclined to the more tedious follow through.

But lots of people are so inclined. They track what they eat, or how they move. They register the places they go during the day using their cellphones, record their mood changes, rate the restaurants they've eaten in, track the length and pace of their runs. You can do it too: you can sign up for any number of online services, many of them free, that let you track the movies you've watched, the purchases you've made, the routes you've walked, or the beverages you've consumed. As the saying goes, there's an app for that. More and more of us are keeping track of the statistical minutiae of daily life, leading lives that are increasingly numerically documented. But why? What is the particular pleasure in seeing daily experience converted into numbers?

So, out of curiosity, and in spite of my lack of attention to detail, I decided to experiment with tracking my ordinary, banal, everyday habits. I did it for about a year, over the course of working on this book, though I'm the first to admit that I was far from rigorous or systematic. Mostly, I wanted to understand why self-tracking was a growing phenomenon, and perhaps along the way, I would understand more about myself. Maybe seeing my life expressed numerically would show me things that the subjective story I like to tell myself wouldn't. My profile showed everything from the exercise I'd been doing, to the lunches I'd brought to work, to the books I'd read, unfolding over time, or displayed in a pie chart of appealing or appalling clarity. I came to think of it as my Data Map, a digital, statistical version of my real, physical life. We are a culture drunk on numbers, and I too was becoming besotted.

This new social habit of tracking our daily behaviours, routines, bodily functions, tastes, and preferences is fuelled in part by our tools. Digital technology makes it easy – and fun – to engage in this tracking. What would once have been an unwieldy and bizarre commitment to personal information–gathering is now a casual and painless process. At the same time, there are psychological and social factors at work, pushing us to track our moves, and some of those factors are troubling. There can be a compulsive aspect to the practice. In part, this reflects our North American culture of relentless scheduling and our ideology of self-improvement. It's also a sign of a broader problem that affects contemporary digital culture in particular. For all its pleasures and benefits, digital life fundamentally time-shifts and place-shifts us out of the here and now. It is precisely this disembodied, distracted, digital life we lead, I argue, that is creating the urge to document the physical body.

This phenomenon of digital self-reporting comes bundled with very real, pressing issues of privacy. Though we charge ahead with this voluminous documentation of our lives, we haven't adequately addressed yet what can be done with this information, such as how and with whom to share it, or how we can anonymize it to shield personally identifying information.

These are large and, to say the least, worrisome caveats, but the growing boom in self-tracking is exciting nevertheless. For while it seems trivial – silly, even – what is remarkable about self-tracking is the surprising power it offers. At the personal level, it can help us change behaviour, but it also offers insight, providing us with an undeniably clear picture of how we behave. And, really, who among us is not looking for insight into what makes us tick? Ultimately, though, the real value of this self-generated data comes in the aggregate. Pooled with other individuals' data, our information offers insight into the broader world. The dream is that we can reveal insights about group behaviour, in the same way my pedometer reveals things about my individual behaviour. That digital record of our individual experience, repeated over and over with countless citizens, can offer insight into everything from where to eat dinner tonight to how diseases are spreading. Properly anonymized, aggregate information about group behaviour can help us plan better, allowing us to make our cities more sustainable, efficient, and responsive. This dream is not a luxury reserved for the developed world, either. Already, being able to track the location of people's cellphones is helping decision-makers understand how urban planning decisions are affecting slums in Rwanda, and how malaria resources can be used more effectively in Kenya, to name just two examples. Now that most of the world's cellphone subscribers live in developing countries, their phone data can give those societies in particular vital demographic information.[1]

I can imagine what you're probably thinking right now: that self-tracking is the kind of behaviour that neurotics and narcissists engage in, a sort of digital scab-picking that most people wouldn't dream of. If you think you don't engage in this self-tracking, though, consider this. The people who track how many steps they take, who monitor sleep quality and create charts of how productive they were at work, are the thin edge of a wedge that broadens to include a widespread cultural urge to "auto-report," to document the self.

What is posting status updates on Facebook if not a sort of ritualized documentary practice that you freely share with others, a way of taking the shifting moments of mood and behaviour and preference and activity and staking them to the ground? The self-tracking phenomenon extends beyond tracking what our bodies are doing to tracking the way we interact with the world around us – dubbed "interaction with environment" tracking, by data visualization expert Nathan Yau.[2] Toting up experiences – the places we've visited, the books we've read, the people we've met, and the restaurants we've dined in – the logging of daily routines on Facebook – comes from the same impulse to document ourselves, to create a digital track record. Maybe you remember when Facebook first opened up to the general public, when it seemed bizarre that people would want to post and share everyday "what I had for lunch" information with others. That, too, may have seemed narcissistic, before perfectly ordinary people started to see the benefits of the casual sharing of the banal details of one's life. Because it is so easy to do, this sort of auto-reportage may soon become as consistent and complete as the most dedicated self-tracker's record. The data we generate about ourselves is stuff we *choose* to track. All the same, in an increasingly digital world, merely going about our daily lives generates digital trails about our behaviour. The more digital our lives, the more complete the Data Map.

My hope is that by talking about this rapidly emerging future we can start to shape it, on both a personal and a political level. As individuals, we need to use these tracking tools critically and consciously. Used properly, they offer us the chance to truly listen to the body, and to reground ourselves in the here and now. But if we use them improperly, we risk surrendering ourselves to the disembodied, distracted self so many of us struggle with in the digital world already. Politically, we can either accept passively what our data will be used for, or we can participate in defining the values we want our data collection to serve.

We are at the dawn of a watershed change in the amount of data out there about us. It is created by us, about us. The stakes are high: will we use it for personal insight, and to build smarter, more sustainable communities, or will we use it for control, surveillance, and profit? Only by understanding the revolution already underway can we debate where we want it to go.

This is a book about technology, in a way, but these are not really technical questions. The questions are about what it means to be a self in the digital world, and what it means to be a citizen. They are questions that are more political – and more spiritual – than technical. This is not a discussion to be handed over to technocrats; it's a discussion for humans, and for citizens.

# ONE

# AN ACCOUNTANT FOR THE BODY
## The Culture of Self-Tracking

Meet Nicholas Felton. Nicholas is a graphic artist and information designer based in New York City. He's also a self-tracker. I've only spoken to Nicholas a couple of times, once for my radio show, Spark, and once while researching this book. Nonetheless, I know a lot about him. In 2008, Nicholas walked an average of 3.13 miles per day. That same year, he bought five items of clothing from China, and only one from Canada (I'd put money on it being a Canada Goose parka). During those twelve months, he went to one poker night, but visited a museum seven times. I know all this because since 2005 Nicholas has been publishing The Feltron Annual Report, a compendium of statistical minutiae about his daily life, displayed in the kind of eye-candy graphics you'd expect from a New York designer. Besides being lovely, it's surprisingly revelatory. I mean, it says something about a guy that he goes to museums seven times as often as he plays poker.

The funny thing is, *The Feltron Annual Report* is actually quite popular, and by that I mean popular with people besides Nicholas Felton. Lots of folks – people who don't even know Nicholas – enjoy studying how many beverages he consumed or how much time he spent playing a video game. When I spoke to Nicholas in 2010, he told me his website receives hundreds of thousands of visitors each year. The popularity of the *Report* goes beyond idle websurfing, too. According to Nicholas, about 2,000 people typically buy physical copies of each of his reports, even though you can look at it online for free. Sure, many of his readers may be drawn to his beautiful infographics as much as fascinated by the details of his life, but it's a remarkable response all the same to a document that ought to be (sorry, Nicholas) dull.

Nicholas may be at the extreme end when it comes to self-tracking, but he's hardly alone in wanting to track his behaviour. He even co-founded (along with Ryan Case) Daytum.com, for other self-trackers to use. It's a website that allows anyone to collect this kind of information about herself, and then, with a couple of mouse clicks, display that information as really snappy-looking lists, charts, or graphs in pretty colours. I used it myself, over the course of writing this book. As the website describes it, it's designed to help you "collect, categorize and communicate your everyday data." You decide what you want to track, although the focus is on the kind of ephemera that we don't normally trouble ourselves about. If you use (as I did) the free version of Daytum, your information is public; anyone can peruse the intimate, if ordinary, details of users' lives. It sounds odd, but in fact, using websites such as Daytum.com is becoming surprisingly normal.

### TRACKING THE ROOTS OF SELF-TRACKING

The phenomenon I'm describing goes by many names. I call it self-tracking, but others have dubbed it self-monitoring, self-surveillance, personal metrics, or used the wonderfully evocative phrase "The Quantified Self." For our purposes, it means, in its strictest sense, keeping a record of information about yourself, in a format that can be expressed in a statistical way. This is self-understanding by numbers, facts, or objective updates, not the free-form self-scrutiny or reportage of the diarist or blogger. The other main feature of self-tracking is how common it is to share that information with others via online services. I'm not talking about the confessional culture of over-sharing on Facebook, or of people anonymously blogging about the intimate details of their lives. For the most part, self-tracking isn't about recording things others would find salacious or disturbingly personal. It's the ordinary, even trivial, bits of information we're generating as we go about our daily lives. Some of this is data we're making a conscious effort to capture and track, just as Nicholas Felton does in his annual report; some of it, such as the geographic location of the cellphone we're carrying, is information that we generate passively simply through our use of current digital technology, but which nonetheless reveals a lot about how we are spending our time.

In some ways, the idea of self-tracking is an old one. The concept of pedometers, for instance, goes back at least as far as da Vinci, and our common notion of the pedometer for personal fitness was in popular use in Japan in the 1960s. In the research world, for years, there's been work on medical technologies that allow people with chronic medical conditions to more easily, even automatically, monitor their health by using electronic devices.

Something started to change, though, once our everyday environment became digitized and networked and once regular, non–technically minded people had access to digital tools, not just to look up information, or to correspond via email, but to share digital information with others. Some digitally engaged people had long been posting their own information to the Web, of course, building their own websites or participating in communities of shared interest, but by 2005 or so it started to be easier for ordinary people to do things like post photos to Flickr or videos to YouTube, put status updates on Facebook or Twitter, write blogs, and to use these tools to connect to friends or like-minded strangers online. As websites designed to help us post information took off, they encouraged us to share more and more details about our lives, and to consider it quite ordinary to do so. I first started noticing that this trend might go far beyond casually sharing photos or thoughts to become an almost obsessive self-documentation when "life-caching" – documenting and sharing as much of one's life digitally as one could, and sharing it with others – became a bit of a buzzword back in 2005. However, it remained a bleeding-edge concept rather than an actual pop-culture trend. A few years later, news stories about portable devices for tracking performance started popping up – watches, electronic performance coaches, training tools for athletics geeks. Tracking behaviour was still a fringe activity; like a piece of a jigsaw puzzle, it was waiting for the right pieces to connect with so that the full picture could emerge.

For self-tracking to really take off, it had to be easy. New digital tools have made it simple both to record what we're doing, and to share that information in elegant, convenient ways. More and more of us have cellphones, and in particular, smart phones, equipped with GPS, that "know" where they are and have cameras and keypads for easy info updates. The "app revolution" has made it easy to document highly specific types of information without having to invest in a new device. Finally, data visualization tools have sprung up to help keep track of all that information. You don't need to be an Excel warrior to translate raw data into useful information. There are plenty of inexpensive or free online tools to do it for you. As Gary Wolf, a contributing editor at *Wired* magazine and an early documenter of the self-tracking phenomenon, describes the conditions for the self-tracking trend in "The Data-Driven Life":

> Then four things changed. First, electronic sensors got smaller and better. Second, people started carrying powerful computing devices, typically disguised as mobile phones. Third, social media made it seem normal to share everything. And fourth, we began to get an inkling of the rise of a global superintelligence known as the cloud.[1]

Once all these factors came together, the technological pre-conditions for a full-on trend were in place.

Apart from our technological readiness, we've also started to think differently about what these personal statistics tell us, and about what they can do for us. The author and journalist Anand Giridharadas has called ours the Age of Metrics,[2] to refer, in part, to our love of personal statistics. Giridharadas argues that we are fascinated by what analytics show us or, at least, by what they purport to show us. We have faith that adding up numbers and subjecting them to the stern truth of analytics will produce inarguable facts that we can use to change our lives.

## THEY'RE KEEPING TRACK OF WHAT?

What are people tracking? Everything, basically. If you can think of a behaviour to track, you can probably find people who are tracking it, and a website that facilitates it. Sales of the popular Fitbit, a wearable device that tracks movement and sleep patterns, were so strong that Fitbits were on back order for months after they came on the market. There are websites to track your fluctuating mood, your sleep habits, your exercise patterns, and even the people you had sex with (including how long it lasted, and how it was for you – rated with a star system!) Location-based tracking – done by checking in on services such as Foursquare.com, or through GPS-fuelled mapping of hikes, runs, and tourist sights visited – is an increasingly popular subset of self-tracking. In 2010, Foursquare grew by more than 3,000 per cent,[3] the same year Facebook launched its own self-check-in service, Places.

The clearest example, though, of the culture of self-tracking, and where you can find its most self-reflective, mature expression, can be found at QuantifiedSelf.com. This online community, maintained by Gary Wolf, Alexandra Carmichael, and the technology guru Kevin Kelly, tracks self-tracking techniques. It's a place to share techniques with others and to acquire, as they say at the website, "self-knowledge through self-tracking." The site attracts people who are interested in using metrics to evaluate the impacts of their personal behaviours. The Quantified Self vibe reminds me a little of the "gentlemen scientists" of the Victorian Era: they are dedicated amateurs conducting research on themselves, gathering data and testing hypotheses, with an eye to not only achieving better performance but to gaining insight that they can then share with others, online as well as in an ongoing series of real world "meet-ups" in cities across North America and internationally. There's a charming geek sensibility that runs through it, with people trying to make deductions, based on personal statistics, about how to live better. A Quantified Self-er might, for instance, want to track how well he slept on a series of nights and then correlate that data with what he ate, his mood, or how much exercise he got, to try and figure out what combination of lifestyle behaviours makes for the best night's sleep. Like those Victorians, too, the Quantified Self-er has a love of new technologies, and shares considerable information about new tools for self-tracking and techniques of data display and analytics. The Quantified Self community is the intellectual hobbyist's version of self-tracking, a sort of subculture of people who take this stuff seriously. I think it's a bellwether, though, of where the culture is headed.

To learn more about how the Quantified Self-ers think about their project, I contacted Carlos Rizo, one of the organizers of Quantified Self Toronto. He trained as a physician but his primary focus now is what he calls "health innovation," working at "the intersection of medicine, technology, and personal improvement," so he seemed like the perfect person to consider self-tracking as a personal and social phenomenon. We met on a sunny spring day, having coincidentally rolled up to the same bike stand at the same time, and before we started chatting, he entered data about his bike ride on his phone (I make a mental note to add the less precise "one short bike ride" to my online tracking profile).

Rizo got interested in self-tracking because of a personal crisis. In 2006, after a serious accident, he became a full-time patient for several years. As both a patient and a physician, he tells me, he turned his attention to his healing process. He began by tracking his pain, figuring out how to characterize and qualify his pain more finely, as a response to the fact that his medication wasn't working as well as it might. Now, though, he tracks his steps, calories, bike rides, what he's eating, the places he visits, "as a way to understand who I am, and to be able to see it." Using the tools of self-tracking as a way to understand himself better is something Rizo sees as a conscious strategy: "It's, in a way, a game, a game we play with ourselves to learn about ourselves."

The common knock on self-tracking is that people are monitoring their lives instead of simply living them, but Rizo doesn't see it that way. Self-tracking is a way to connect more deeply to himself and his body: "It's a way to awaken . . . your gut, awaken your sense of 'this is what I feel,' this is what my body's telling me . . . [for example] my body's telling me that I need to be more responsible about what I am putting in my mouth." I love that idea of using technology to awaken your body's knowledge about itself, and it squares with my own experience of self-tracking leading to greater awareness. In a world of zeroes and ones, where so much of our lives are virtual, self-tracking – when used with the kind of consciousness Rizo suggests – can bring us back to the physical reality of the body.

### "HERO OF THE BEACH": CHARLES ATLAS 2.0

Though The Quantified Self folks may be the geek elite of this nascent movement, most people who self-track have almost certainly never heard of them. The most obvious place self-tracking has gone mainstream is in tracking the physical body, where self-tracking is less of a consciously thought-out strategy toward life and personal experimentation and more of an expression of athletic performance culture, where even recreational athletes have a ton of gear and expertise.

You're probably already familiar with popular examples of fitness tracking, such as the Nike+ system. It tracks how far and how quickly you run, using a little accelerometer in your shoe, which knows how long your foot has been on the ground and hence how quickly you're running. An additional tool arrived in the fall of 2010, when Nike introduced the Nike+ GPS app, which allows users to track their pace and map their runs on their iPhones. They create a profile at Nikeplus.com, so that the information the app tracks can be synced to it. It's a smart way to bring together location-awareness technologies, the booming app world, and – something we'll see a lot of – devices such as smart phones that know how and where they are being used.

Nike+ was early to the self-tracking game, hitting the shelves in 2006. Since then, track-your-fitness technologies have exploded. The Web is rich with services to help us lose weight and stay fit through recording our diet and exercise, but the success of apps for phones and the availability of relatively inexpensive mobile devices have brought us a panoply of wearable tools too. Because I am cheap, I used regular old-school pedometers to track my kilometres, but really, this is incredibly outmoded. Motion capture grows more sophisticated all the time. Devices such as the Fitbit use the same 3D-motion sensors as do gaming devices such as the Wii. This means you can capture data that is more "fine-grained," evaluating things such as how long you are sleeping and how long it took you to fall asleep. Unlike my Daytum recording, where I have to remember to enter my data, with systems such as the Fitbit, all you need to do is bring your device close to its docking station, and that information is automatically uploaded to your online profile – the data is captured for you. Using some of these tools can even create a sort of feedback loop, for example, Adidas's MiCoach, a running tracking app, offers words of encouragement based on the stats you're generating. I suspect these trackers will look primitive in a few years as self-tracking grows more automatic and more sophisticated. These programs are part of the scientization of physical culture and the body, which takes a discourse that was once the preserve of elite performance athletes and generalizes it to us weekend warriors. The sophistication of these tools amounts to a professionalization of what might once have been informal self-tracking.

The other most striking place we see the self-tracking boom, alongside the athletics-based tracking devices, is in calorie-counting and weight loss, with an astonishing number of websites designed to help users track calories consumed and burned. Given the size of the diet industry, it's perhaps no surprise that the people who design sites find dieters an appealing target. These sites are a natural market for targeted weight-loss advertising, which often supports the free services. Dieters open an account at one of these sites in order to use self-reportage and frequent check-ins, the Web 2.0–era equivalent of the Weight Watchers weigh-in, to help them manage their weight. Sites such as FitDay.com, DailyBurn.com, and My-calorie-counter.com let you track your weight, exercise, and calorie consumption in order to reach your goals. Some of these online diaries allow users to easily share their progress or setbacks with others and to have something of an online support group. Of course, unlike a face-to-face Weight Watchers' group, it relies strictly on the individual's word about what she or he weighs.

Technological innovation means it's easier than ever to track calories and subject your food intake to scrutiny. Take the Thin Cam app, for instance. It lets you take pictures of your food with your phone and upload those yummy snaps to the Thin-site.com website, all the better to track your calories. The premise is that the constant capturing of what you are actually putting in your mouth will make you more mindful of what you're eating. Intuitively, this seems like the kind of thing that would work. I imagine I'd be much less likely to eat that second piece of pie if I had to go through the step of taking a picture of it, never mind be confronted with the documentary evidence of my over-indulgence later. Being aware of what you are actually doing is one of the first steps in many types of behaviour change. Anyone who has ever tried to lose weight knows that not deceiving yourself in what you're actually eating is an important step, and dieters have long kept food-consumption diaries. From the outside, though, you can't help but feel that there's a relentlessly joyless quality to this sort of self-tracking. Sources of bodily delight and physical expressiveness, such as running or eating a meal, are reduced to stats-driven, objectified activities.

While we may benefit from filling in our information and tracking our stats, the sites where we log our data benefit too. Online services may obtain information that's helpful in selling more targeted ads, sure, but the insights can be more surprising than that. Nike+, for instance, has access to information about things like the average length of time people run at various times of the year, or the most popular workout songs.[4] Even if that information is logged anonymously, it still may be useful to Nike. Wouldn't it help Nike to, say, craft popular ad campaigns if its marketing team knew what sort of music was inspiring its most dedicated runners and best customers, and when?

## SIMPLE TOOLS TO TRACK AND MEET GOALS

While fitness or weight-loss sites are natural homes for self-trackers, they are just one category among the many online services directed toward people accomplishing a goal, any goal. Beeminder.com, for instance, takes an interesting motivational spin on this idea. It allows you to define your goal and report your stats, then in effect coaches you through achieving your goal by displaying your progress as an overall trend rather than as a disheartening series of daily ups and downs. You can choose whatever goal you like, but it needs to be, as they say, something that "you can put a periodic number on." That is, you can track any behaviour you want, from losing weight to writing a book, but, as for many of these services, your goals must be structured around a goal which can be numerically quantified. Of course, this means that anything that can't be assigned a "periodic number" risks falling off the table.

Self-tracking techniques can even be used to study mental well-being too. Again, there are lots of tools that allow you to do this, not just in order to look back at how you were feeling over a period of months, but also to try and make a correlation between how you feel and what is going on in your life, with an eye to learning about what triggers your anxieties or depressions. A sign that this self-tracking of interior states is being taken seriously appeared in the autumn of 2010, when the US Army announced the winners of its "app" competition, one of which was the Telehealth Mood Tracker, which helps soldiers track the range of their emotions and moods when they are in stressful, to say the least, situations.

Self-tracking extends the idea of performance and improvement beyond the purely physical arena to behavioural improvement more generally. Once you start to think of your body as a site of observation and experimentation, you can think of your daily activities this way too. Self-trackers might monitor books read, movies seen, work habits, or any activity that they want to improve. One of the most popular tools for this kind of behaviour modification is Mint.com, the popular personal-finance website. Users upload their financial information – including the username and password they use for Web banking – and report on where, when, and how much money they're spending, all in the aid of creating and sticking to budgets for themselves. And you don't need to manually record every time you went to the bank machine, either – it's automatically noted on your profile for you. This increasingly automatic capturing of self-tracking information is another hallmark of the trend.

Mint.com is an example of the structured personal-betterment-through-observation approach that's typical of much of self-tracking; it's a commitment that can be quite rigorous. For instance, as part of my own self-tracking, I experimented with a helpful Internet-era torture device for writers and other computer-bound types, called RescueTime. RescueTime is the kind of service that can be used by managers to track employee productivity. It allows employers to monitor where employees are spending their time on the computer: how much time employees are spending on Facebook instead of Excel spreadsheets, say. It monitors where they go on the Web, how much time they spend answering emails, and what applications they are using on their computers. Leaving aside the question of whether it's ethical or useful to engage in this kind of surveillance, RescueTime also offers *personal* productivity tools, should you want to subject yourself to the same controlling gaze. You list your most and least productive computer-based activities, based on the kind of work you do, and then RescueTime records how long you spend on productive versus unproductive tasks. You are also expected to check in when you have been away from your computer, to indicate what you've been doing (though at least in this case your virtual prison guard allows you a "none of your business" option).

Even for someone like me, who, on a *productive* day, has a job that legitimately involves a fair bit of surfing the Web looking for stuff, this is an absolute horror show, showcasing my stellar ability to procrastinate. There is nothing like returning to the computer after making a cup of tea and seeing a pop-up screen asking you what you have been doing since 9:01. Five minutes and 43 seconds have elapsed. Time when I was supposed to be working! Once a week, RescueTime sends you a helpful little summary in an email, breaking down the activities you've spent time on. I have to admit, RescueTime did help me. I installed it voluntarily, of course, and in doing so, I learned useful things, such as what my distractions are (hello, email!). Its language use was neutral; it didn't hector me. At the same time, though, I hated it. Yes, it gave me insight into what I was doing, and in so doing, provided motivation to change. Yet in turning my daily work into a series of goals to be met and activities to be charted, it made me feel like a hamster on a wheel, and also in some sense an object, rather than a subject, in my own life. There's a distinct whiff of Maoist self-criticism about listing what you believe to be productive and unproductive activities and then arranging for that to be reported back to you. Services such as RescueTime point to another key feature of today's self-tracking: its intensive focus on how we are spending our time. With the advent of self-tracking, we increasingly feel compelled to give a reckoning of how we are spending every minute.

## IT'S EASY . . . BUT DOES IT WORK?

Intuitively, self-tracking as a driver for behaviour change seems like a no-brainer, like it ought to work: I track how productive I am, and so my productivity improves. The funny thing is that the evidence for self-tracking as an effective tool of behaviour change is not entirely persuasive. Alone, the simple act of using self-tracking tools may not be enough to change our actions. To find out what makes self-tracking really effective, I decided to talk to B. J. Fogg. He is founder and director of the Persuasive Technology Lab at Stanford University, and has a background in human-computer interaction. He studies how technologies such as mobile devices can influence behaviour change, and he's been thinking about self-tracking (he calls it "self-monitoring") in this context.

Over the phone, from his office in California, he tells me that in fact it doesn't always work simply to monitor what you're doing, and that many systems "over-rely" on self-monitoring as an approach to making changes in behaviour. In that case, I wondered, how can we build technologies that do support change? Fogg thinks that these strategies of monitoring work best when they are accompanied by other techniques. Tools to help us change our behaviour work best when they track and reward us, but also when they remind us – in Fogg's terminology, "trigger" us – when we're in a position to actually carry out the behaviour. There's not much point in triggering someone to do push-ups when she is driving her car, he offers by way of example.

Fogg thinks the key to linking monitoring to behaviour change lies in this concept of a "trigger." "And with mobile," he tells me, "we're going to get better and better at doing that. Until now, it's been pretty hard." The potential with personal technologies such as cellphones with customized apps is that they can provide feedback, motivation, and little rewards at the exact moments when they will help us change our behaviour. Fogg points out that the kind of feedback that shows us that we are getting better helps us stick to our goals; it's the "secret sauce" that makes video games so compelling. Mobile technologies are a great tool for providing ongoing feedback because they're always with us.

While cellphones help, Fogg says that most cellphone apps are still not where they need to be. Designing a system that really works means not only tying it to his "trigger, track, reward" approach but also making it simple and quick:

> If I have to look up how many calories this thing of yogurt has and specify that it's raspberry and it takes 60 seconds to input that I'm eating a cup of raspberry yogurt, eventually almost everyone will stop doing it . . . for most people it's got to be one click. And that's hard to do but we will get there eventually.

The ready-to-hand mobile technologies that are becoming part of everyday life are going to be a game changer in terms of encouraging people to alter negative behaviours: "The future of persuasion is all about technology," Fogg tells me, "and eventually it's all about mobile. There's just nothing that will compare to it." So, as we start to see cellphone apps and mobile tools take off, self-tracking for behaviour change may become more effective, and more popular, than ever.

## UPDATE: I JUST UPDATED MY STATUS!

I wonder, when people have retro costume parties in twenty years' time, what will the iconic markers be that will telegraph to partygoers that you're "dressed like this decade," in the way that a flapper dress signals the Jazz Age? In addition to the low-riding skinny jeans and the ironic-nerdy glasses, there will surely be some marker of the time in which the "status update" took off as a pop-cultural practice. Whether that's answering "What's on your mind?" on Facebook, or "checking in" on Foursquare, we increasingly engage what I think of as auto-reportage, a continual ticker tape registering how and where you are, and what you're doing.

The humble status update may not at first seem to have much in common with the driven self-betterment of fitness tracking and mood monitoring, but I think it springs from the same source. I include it in self-tracking because it comes from the same drive for a self-reckoning or accounting. Unlike self-tracking for self-improvement – which may be public, or entirely private – the status update doesn't make sense outside of a social context. I think of the status update as a sort of *Horton Hears a Who* means of saying "I am here. I am here!" It's a continual registering of presence, and is, in a sense, a way of being "seen" by others. It's the urge to create the self as a documented, persistent, even curated, object.

Closely linked to the status update is the registering of opinions, tastes, and preferences. People may do this simply as part of their normal status updates, but they may also do so by signing up for services such as Yelp or Urbanspoon that require them to report their reactions to what they experience. While there's no doubt a utility to being able to access someone's pocket restaurant reviews on a service such as Urbanspoon (and no doubt, too, an appeal to the amateur restaurant critic lurking within many of us), at least part of its attraction to people who contribute reviews is that it creates a persistent profile of where the user ate and when and what her observations and experiences were like. As with the status update, this auto-reportage creates a persistent accounting or reckoning of the individual's time and behaviour.

## DIGITAL BRINGS A WHOLE NEW MEANING TO TRACKING THE SELF

Up to this point, I've given examples of things that we explicitly choose to track, but I'd like to range more broadly in thinking about what we mean by self-tracking. Increasingly – and this is a crucial difference from all previous forms of self-tracking and auto-reportage – we are using digital devices, whether they're purpose-built trackers or a general tool such as our app-enriched cellphones. The distinguishing feature of these digital tools is that they know how, when, and often where they are being used. For instance, if I use the Amazon Kindle, it "knows" where I am in my reading of a book. It records what passages I highlighted and any notes I make. If I'm an avid reader and I'm trying to improve the effectiveness of my reading that might be information I want to know about, year on year. Even if I don't, though, this information may be more useful when it's shared with others. Amazon allows readers to share the notes they've made on an e-book with their Public Notes function, or they can learn how other Kindle readers use their books, because Amazon aggregates that information into a "most highlighted" feature. This feature is enabled because readers are highlighting not with a pen but with the device itself, and also because the device continues to have a relationship with Amazon. This type of information is present when we are using our phones, working on our computers, or wearing our Fitbits. In the case of my RescueTime software, I chose to track how I was using my computer, but it might just as easily have been that my employer was tracking how I was using it, without even telling me.

Here, then, is a curious modern twist on the idea of "self"-tracking. Simply by virtue of using digital tools, we are invoking a technology of surveillance of the self. A decision to switch from analog to digital carries with it a decision to have the way you are engaging with a technology registered. As computers evolve from expensive devices that sit on our desks, to bits of computational power dispersed throughout our environment (not just as phones and health monitors, but as sensors out in the world), engaging with digital technology means engaging the potential for gathering and storing digital information, whether we choose to use it or not – in fact, whether we are aware of it or not.

These last two areas of self-tracking – on the one hand, our own repeated reporting of status, of location, of opinion; on the other, the inadvertent tracking of ourselves that goes on simply by virtue of our using digital devices – stretch the definition of self-tracking well beyond the narrow confines of intentional monitoring of behaviour for self-improvement. Certainly, they extend the definition beyond what the folks at The Quantified Self would recognize in what they're doing. I include it for several reasons. As I've already suggested, the status update and the check-in have much in common with other forms of self-tracking, in terms of their emotional and psychological motivation. The inadvertent monitoring that's part and parcel of digital technologies is something that I think we are going to start to tap into a lot more in the future as we realize its power to capture information about our behaviour. More centrally, though, the pattern I see emerging is one where everyday information about where we are going, what we are doing, how we are moving, and how we feel is brought together in the creation of a digital picture of ourselves. It's a picture that combines the intentional and the unintentional. Compiled into a Data Map, it gives us one (though not the only) strong depiction of who we are. The representation of who a person is becomes the vast amount of data the person generates. I think this is potentially transformative, for good and for ill.

## THE STRANGENESS OF NOW

My favourite example of the culture of self-tracking is the "what I ate" people, simply because they bring together four aspects of the self-tracking trend: the detailed, trivial, reportage aspect of self-tracking; the ease of doing so, thanks to portable digital tools; the pleasure of sharing the information with others; and the absolute head-scratching oddness of it to those who don't understand its particular attraction. Just who are the "what I ate" people? They are mostly photo bloggers, who take pictures of their food before they eat it. While I'm pretty sure you could put most of them somewhere on the "foodie" scale, these aren't people who are documenting some high-flying culinary adventure, like a trip to France, or a life-changing meal at The Fat Duck. This is a quotidian record of what people put in their yaps, day in, day out. Although the photographs can often be quite lovingly taken, the fact that pretty much everyone has a cellphone now means that no streetside hot dog, no homemade mac 'n' cheese, need go undocumented; part of the popularity of "what I ate" blogs is just that it's so easy to snap a digital photo and upload it to a website with a few tags about what it is and where it was consumed. The important thing, though, is that there needn't be a lot of context around food photos; we're not talking *Julie and Julia* here, just brute documentation. It's the raw power of blunt data, and photographic evidence.

It's hard to say just how many people are taking pictures of what they eat, although an article on the trend in the *New York Times* points out that one of the biggest groups on the photo-sharing website Flickr is the "I Ate This" group.[5]

(When I checked on it early in 2011, it had over 400,000 photos that more than 23,000 people had taken of meals consumed, ready to share with anyone else who was interested.) It's a significant enough trend that there have been etiquette articles on when and how to take pictures of your food.[6] (Apparently, taking photos discreetly in restaurants is fine, but no flash, and no, uh, tripod.)

It's easy to sit in judgement about self-monitoring, if you don't do it. There is, however, something deeply human about the urge to document our lives, to look back at a pattern of our behaviour and make sense of it, to use it to construct the narrative of our lives. Among our most vivid memories are the moments of anguish, exaltation, or humiliation that are so few and far between for most of us. Perhaps, though, the real narratives of our lives are measured out with coffee spoons. If, as Aristotle said, we are what we repeatedly do, then the story of ourselves may be revealed in the humbler patterns of our behaviour. Beyond the subjective introspection of the heart, the data-mapped self promises a picture that is observable, measurable, quantified, and persistent over time. It is a "me" I can point to, a "me" with graphics.

And yet, it feels as though there is something at risk if the numerical self is taken too far. When I started using RescueTime, for instance, I knew I had seen the future. RescueTime represents a certain kind of vision of capturing data about how you spend your time: it's easy, seamless, and doesn't require much reflection on your part, at least until you are faced with the evidence of your failure to meet the goals you set for yourself. What will it mean to live in such a way that we won't, as it were, have private space away from ourselves? Going about your daily life might become an exercise in performing to expectations. It changes the nature of human agency if I am not just behaving, but responding to an ideal image that I now must measure up to. I imagine our culture in five years, heck, in two years. How luxurious those stolen analog moments will seem, when your phone didn't know that you left work early and wandered the streets lost in thought, when your computer didn't ask you where you were when you returned from a trip to the park or a mid-afternoon movie. Once your devices "know" how they are being used, self-tracking may not require much of an active role on your part; it may just involve saying yes, installing the software, downloading the app, or configuring your email, so that you can be efficient and perfectible. There's no natural limit to it, either. If you are determined to be fitter or more productive, at what point do the numbers and graphs tell you to relax and have some French fries? It's as though we have taken the rigidities of a supervised schoolroom and imposed them on ourselves, in the name of – what, exactly? Of being the best "you" you can be? Or of measuring up to an ideal, a version of ourselves, at the right weight and fitness, marching through our workday, crossing off tasks and keeping track?

# TWO

# WE ARE ALL BEN FRANKLIN NOW
*Why We Self-Track*

Between cool gadgets, online sharing, and the prevalence of digital culture, self-tracking might look like a thoroughly contemporary trend, yet another example of our frenetic response to data deluge, as we spin in ever-tighter circles of digital self-regard. And sure, there are distinctly contemporary reasons why self-tracking is becoming so popular. The roots of personal monitoring, though, actually run deep in Western culture. We have long yearned to have a concrete record of our behaviour, attitudes, and states of being, in order to better ourselves. It's not just that we want to know ourselves, or that we want to be better people; we want to see ourselves at some remove in order to do so.

The technological factors behind self-tracking reach back to long before the digital age, and are, in fact, the product of the culture of print. As print culture developed, the individual became the primary social unit, and this shift was accompanied by a new push toward self-improvement and individual self-making. There are psychological and socio-historical factors, too, behind our centuries-old drive to self-track. We have embraced the self as something that can be studied, pointed to, and refined. Modern culture as a whole has driven us to become disciplined, productive beings, and over time we've come to see that productive, objectified self as the very definition of who we are, a self that can be scrutinized with a scientific and technical gaze. Our love of number crunching our personal data is the latest manifestation of the fundamentally modern, Western, individualist project, taken to its logical, digitally powered conclusion.

## MEET PRODUCTIVITY GURU, BEN FRANKLIN!

Benjamin Franklin could be a perfect model for our technologically fixated times. His *Poor Richard's Almanack*, full of pithy sayings, might have made him a successful blogger today. With his interest in rolling up his sleeves and inventing, he would have been a perfect fit at a Silicon Valley start-up. Fans of our current culture of self-tracking could look to Franklin as an early, analog poster boy: a devotee of documenting, perfecting, and monitoring, on the path to self-improvement.

In his autobiography, Franklin describes taking on "the bold and arduous project of arriving at moral perfection."[1] Suddenly, my efforts to keep track of my bicycle rides look a wee bit underachieving. In keeping with his pragmatic approach to life, Franklin decided that what he needed was a program, a system, to tackle his project in a rational way. He's a bit like a proto–David Allen, the productivity expert particularly popular with tech-y types, whose *Getting Things Done* manifesto advocates breaking down a large project into a series of tasks, thus taming an overwhelmingly large goal, such as, oh, "arriving at moral perfection," by means of a dogged determination simply to do the next thing on the list. More than just deciding to be a better person, Franklin essentially designed a *technology* for meeting his goals. It's his systematic application of technique to moral purification that seems so familiar to us.

Here's what Franklin did, in case you're interested in arriving at moral perfection yourself. First, he made up a list of thirteen distinct virtues, such as temperance, frugality, sincerity, and justice. To track his lapses, and successes, he fashioned a little book. Each page focused on a different virtue. Across the top of the page, he listed the days of the week, and down the side, the thirteen virtues. Each time he sinned against a virtue, he would put a black mark in his little table, toting them up at the end of the day. In order to divide the perfecting process into manageable chunks (another top tip of productivity experts), he focused on one virtue at a time, strenuously making an effort to avoid any errors, any black marks. With the other virtues, meanwhile, he would simply record the evidence of his lapses. This passive accounting of his behaviour with respect to the remaining twelve virtues is the eighteenth-century analog equivalent of our digital tools, whereby we automatically calculate the distance and speed of our runs and beam that information from docking station to website for later examination and trend-spotting. Franklin's goal was to work through each virtue in turn, keeping the particular virtue under scrutiny free of damning black marks, until the page with the last virtue on it was entirely blank, free of any moral lapses. Then he'd go through the whole shebang again. Lather, rinse, repeat.

Franklin writes, "I should be happy in viewing a clean book, after a thirteen weeks' daily examination."[2] I should think you would, after a gruelling thirteen weeks like that. The satisfaction Franklin appears to derive from a sense of improvement is a familiar feeling to us; it's the pleasure not only of making the effort but also in sitting back and observing our accomplishments (and Franklin didn't even have the benefit of sleek websites and snappy graphics).

Franklin went further in self-perfection through self-tracking. Hard as it is to believe of a person who would hatch a scheme like this in the first place, Franklin felt he faced a particular challenge with the virtue of Order, so, according to his autobiography, he designed a "scheme of employment" of a full day. It is simple, yet structured. From 5 a.m. to 8 a.m., he would prepare for the day, eat breakfast, and do something called "address Powerful Goodness!" He would work from 8 a.m. to 6 p.m., with a two-hour break in the middle of the day. Evening would be filled with organization and leisure. Both morning and evening he would make time for an examination of the day (either the one that lay ahead or the one that had just concluded), summed up by the questions "What good shall I do this day/What good have I done to-day?" It's a ritual that seemed to totter between effective self-regulation and a fussy sort of neuroticism. Ultimately, Franklin says he never conquered Order and, sensibly, he decided to live with that as an aspect of his character, thinking himself in any case better for having put in the effort. Over time, he became less rigorous with his recording, but "I always carried my little book with me."[3] Franklin was nothing if not a pragmatist. I wonder if we will all be so capable of living with our failings, as we look at the digital record of our own behaviour.

## TWENTY-FIRST-CENTURY FRANKLINS: THE DIGITAL TURN

In many ways, Franklin's methodical approach is a how-to guide for today's self-tracker. Franklin employed a system (his little book, and the methodology of black marks and individual virtues). He also engineered feedback systems: his twice-daily reflection on how he met or failed to meet his goal of goodness and his regular check-in with the damning evidence of black marks on his book's pages. He shares with contemporary self-trackers the focused need to record and reflect on his progress, not only toward his ultimate goal, but also day to day, as he moves relentlessly toward the target of perfection throughout his thirteen-week morality cleanse.

Franklin's vision for himself, however, was grounded in a different sense of the purpose of self-tracking. Rooted in "moral perfection," and in his idea of "Goodness," Franklin's emphasis was on virtues such as Order, Resolution, Industry, and Cleanliness. He was a Deist, and so giving a moral account of himself may have been a response to not believing in a God who judges human acts and sins. In today's culture of self-tracking, we don't track our morality or our status in achieving Goodness; in fact, I'm fairly certain that after the moral prissiness of the "tween" years, this sort of documentation of moral health would be considered simply neurotic by most North Americans. Instead – and this is truly telling – our tracking is mostly physical. We track the physical movement of our body, and what we put into it; we account for the use of our time day in, day out. There's a reassuring concreteness to it – the body has heft; the clock marks the unfailing passage of time. It's the kind of blunt information that can be registered in external acts rather than by interior moral states. It doesn't require an introspective turn and an examination of the human heart. Franklin must have had to engage in introspection, looking into his heart and pondering, for example, whether he had really acted with sincerity when he answered the third of his personal letters on such and such a day. Our love of objective, statistical information isn't going to help us assess breaches against "justice" or other squishy, hard-to-quantify goals.

This goal of objective evaluation is the norm even when we are tracking states of being rather than activities. The website MoodTracker.com, for instance, is designed to help people dealing with depression and bipolar disorder. It tracks variables such as anxiety levels, and mild, moderate, or severe depression levels, and correlates them with users' reports of how much they slept and changes in their medication. MoodTracker obviously requires users to be aware of their internal states and to report them, but the whole purpose of the exercise is to quantify those states, to render them into something remedied by external, objective factors. This is, of course, an eminently sensible way of trying to make a health condition more manageable, and as someone who has her own struggles with anxiety, I can certainly see why it could be helpful to correlate mood with the external factors that might be influencing it. The one thing it isn't, though, is genuinely introspective. Indeed, the whole point is to manage one's interior state by making it more objectively observable, by externalizing it.

And yet, in spite of these differences, Franklin's self-tracking looks remarkably familiar. If he is more concerned with his moral state, and we with our heart rates, the idea of creating a technology to track what is quicksilver and hidden about our lives and behaviours, and to make it visible, is of a piece with how we approach self-tracking. We share with him an understanding of the self as a project to be undertaken and observed. It feels fundamentally modern, this exercise in self-improvement, in self-making. If it is "modern" to aim for this personal, individual betterment, our self-tracking also shares with Franklin's the drive toward a sort of personal accountancy. This is perhaps what is most familiar to us about Franklin's little book; the drive to document the self, to create a vision of ourselves we can refer to, track, and evaluate.

Julie Rak is a professor in the Department of English and Film Studies at the University of Alberta with a special interest in the diary form, and I called her to get a better understanding of how diary culture arose in the West. Her take is that "Ben Franklin in particular thought that you could perfect yourself," and that the link between diary-keeping and a secular perfectability is distinctly American. It certainly feels as though we are inheritors of a very North American sense of self-improvement, conceived of as a kind of hygiene.

## DEAR DIARY: TODAY, I TRACKED MYSELF

Whether we're looking back at Ben Franklin's book or thinking about our own digital exercises in self-tracking, the diary form is the familiar common denominator. The personal diary serves as a way of keeping track of or recording a persistent sense of who one is, in a form that may be revisited later. When we think of diaries now, we tend to think of them in their private, confessional, "dear diary" form, but historically diaries had a much more public function. They were sometimes personal and yet not necessarily private. Perhaps our current online culture of sharing – and oversharing – is not so unique after all. Diaries have a long and cross-cultural history and took on many forms, so I won't attempt to be exhaustive in documenting the range of styles of personal journals. In the Western tradition, at least, there is even a long history of the sort of moral accountancy Franklin engaged in. When Ancients such as the Stoics examined their consciences, however, they did so internally. In *On Diary*, a collection of his writings, Philippe Lejeune, a leading academic expert in the diary form, writes that you can find references to people scrutinizing their consciences – as Pythagoras does in the sixth century BCE – but you won't find the linking of personal scrutiny to writing one's observations down. The elementary roots of tracking one's moral life in written form began to emerge – in the West, at least – with the early Christians (such as St. Augustine's *Confessions*), and developed through the Middle Ages.[4]

According to Lejeune, we can find the roots of European journals in accounting books and in "family books" kept by merchants in Florence in the fourteenth century.[5] These are examples of what we might think of as proto–self-tracking: straightforward records of what happened, more in keeping with logs or accounts, than our contemporary notion of "diary." The real bedrock of the modern diary goes back to the seventeenth century in the West. This is the era of Samuel Pepys's diary, of course, but also of the so-called Commonplace Book as common cultural practice.

Julie Rak tells me that Commonplace Books were kept in the seventeenth century (though their roots extend back to an earlier time). A Commonplace Book was a place to record observations, list the people who came to call, and also to jot down sayings, morally edifying comments, and the like. It wasn't, unlike our contemporary concept of the diary, intended to be a purely private form. An individual would have her own Commonplace Book, but people who came to call on her might write their own observations or quotations in it too.

However, the diary, and with it our modern notion of personal accounting, really took off when a set of powerful technological innovations made it possible to track what we were doing in a way that was relatively easy and available (sound familiar?). Julie Rak tells me that the fact that the clock, the account book, and the calendar were all standardized in the eighteenth century drove the adoption of diary-keeping.

Philippe Lejeune comments that it "was only in the second half of the eighteenth century that time took on a form close to the one we now know. . . . Keeping a diary is clearly related to this revolution."[6] He notes that "the practice of keeping a *personal* journal emerged in Europe between the late Middle Ages and the eighteenth century, at the same time as the mechanical clock was being developed, on the one hand, and in conjunction with the appearance of the annual calendar and the datebook on the other."[7]

According to Laurie McNeill – also a scholar of the diary form, at the University of British Columbia – as use of the clock and the calendar became more commonplace in the eighteenth century, a sense of personal accounting naturally followed suit. "Once we became able to record time, we became interested in how we were using it," she tells me over the phone. And further, "Once you have a self and a life that should be lived valuably, you need to account for it."

More people began to have access to "print literacy," particularly thanks to the greater availability of paper, and not surprisingly, says Rak, this is also the time when we start to see the arrival of silent reading. Rak notes that there's a link between the rise of diaries and the creation of what we think of as the modern self: "It changes the idea of what your self is. It is possible to be a self that keeps secrets." The individual, regulated self, capable of keeping secrets, and giving a personal account of the self, starts to come into full flower. Philippe Lejeune offers us a particularly extreme example of the benefits of paper in self-tracking. He recounts Saint John Climacus's visits to a religious community in the seventh century AD. The saint observed, amazed, that the monks walked around with tablets attached to their belts. They would write down their thoughts and later give an "exact accounting to the abbot." "Tablets attached to the belt," Lejeune writes, "are perhaps not the best means of keeping a journal."[8] Never mind the effect of the clattering tablets on the serenity of the monastery.

When it comes to the diary, even the more exacting types of self-scrutiny and inward regard were not typically private, in the way we think of it today, until relatively recently. According to Laurie McNeill, people in England, and later, in France, used to keep spiritual diaries, which were a combination of objective record-keeping about spiritual practice and subjective accounts of one's spiritual life. As with Ben Franklin, monitoring and accounting for the self extended beyond the minutiae of how one was spending one's time to matters that were obviously of the utmost importance. In France, though, these spiritual diaries were always intended to be read by a (male) religious guide, and were seen as a way of asking, as she put it, "How can you improve yourself in the eyes of God?" Here, self-tracking was linked to introspection and betterment, and also to bringing oneself closer to God. A far cry from counting your steps with a pedometer.

It was only in the mid-nineteenth century that keeping a diary started to look like our familiarly confessional practice. McNeill tells me we can attribute this in part to the emerging idea of the self as "singular, autonomous and private" and then later, to the rise of psychoanalysis, which brought with it the idea of a self that was not only private but half-submerged, not even entirely knowable to itself, at least not without the rigorous examination of analysis. What seems still so new and strange to us – publicly sharing so much previously private information about oneself – is perhaps not so odd after all, given that our sense of what is really "private" is relatively new.

## THE DRIVE TO DOCUMENT:
## TIME MANAGEMENT AND THE PRODUCTIVE SELF

Our contemporary project of accounting for and recording our individual behaviours is really a continuation of a centuries' old way of thinking about oneself in relation to time, made new with the widespread availability of tools to track that relationship. We've seen how, hundreds of years ago, the wider availability of paper, clocks, and calendars made it possible to keep accounts. Today, inexpensive small sensors, cellphones, social media, and affordable data storage, as Gary Wolf has observed,[9] are our own versions of paper, clocks, and calendars. They make what once might have been an intensive, or very odd, personal commitment, an easy, off-the-shelf hobby. The technology doesn't *cause* the behaviour, but it does come preloaded with a bias toward recording and sharing personal data.

To Wolf's list, I would add a fifth technological component: the rise of tools for the micro-measurement of productivity and time. Forget the humble calendar and clock. New technologies fuel a truly relentless record-keeping of how we spend our time. Like hamsters on the wheel, many of us struggle to keep pace with the deluge of communication and information that comes our way, thanks to digital technology. And so we turn to digital technology and the parcelling out of time into ever-shorter increments to manage that deluge. It may be that the linear, industrial economy of the twentieth century, governed by the time card, is receding, and being replaced by the asynchronous, always-on, post-industrial economy that many of us are entering. Regardless, the marshalling of time into ever-tighter bits has not disappeared. What's surely the most striking characteristic of Ben Franklin's "scheme of employment," for instance, is how little he actually scheduled into his day. For an office worker today, a workday template designating a four-hour block of time as simply "work" would suggest an unmanageable, yawning abyss, sure to be swamped by a wave of distractions. If the clock was an impetus to record-keeping for our self-tracking foremothers and forefathers, how much more pressing is the drive propelling us to keep track of how we are spending our time, in an era when every minute of many people's lives is packaged and accounted for? Just as reading our grandparents' diaries might give us an idea of how they spent their time (when they were unwell, who came to visit, and what the crops were like one particular September), performing a search through many people's online calendars would turn up tightly managed, searchable databases of exactly how those people had spent their time and with whom. If, as McNeill suggests, the ability to record time leads to an interest in accounting for it, it is no wonder we are compelled by the idea of tracking our activities, of micro-managing ourselves. The funny thing is, we are willing not just to have this measurement and constant tracking put upon us, by employers, for example, but to engage in it ourselves. This sense of being relentlessly productive is something we bring not just to our workplaces, but to our lives more generally. The drive to be productive is not just about the online calendar or RescueTime but about the enterprise of turning ourselves into disciplined crea- tures. This is a legacy we share with Ben Franklin and our ancestors who lived by the clock and the account book. It may not be new, but our tools sure do up the ante.

## EVERYONE LIKES A GOLD STAR

The technological factors of data storage and digital tools and time management are not the only forces pushing us to track. There is an undeniable pleasure in it, and this, too, is not new. Just think of Franklin's pleasure in surveying his little notebook. It's funny, but the more you start to monitor the minutiae of your life, the more you find things to track. Personally, I admit, I was a pretty shabby self-tracker in the early going: I'd forget, mostly, or couldn't be bothered. Once I started to get into it though, it was fun, and kind of addic- tive. I started to see the world around me, and the ordinary daily experience of what I did, what I felt, and what I observed around me, on a kind of meta-level. There was the pleasing ritual of adding my stats from the previous day, for instance, or periodically perusing the graphs that summed up how my time was being spent. I started to look for new things that could be tracked. If it could be tracked, that meant it had, if not a pattern, then at least some sort of continuity over time. For instance, fairly early on, I got into tracking how much I was walking and cycling every day. These are pretty typical things for people to track. They are physical, clearly measurable, and linked to a behavioural change a person wants to make: getting more exercise. Over a period of a few days on my early morning walks and my bike rides, I saw animals: a fox, a few groundhogs, a skunk (okay, the skunk was road kill, but I still saw it). This is pretty unusual for someone living in the heart of downtown in Canada's biggest city, so I started tracking "notable wildlife." I would get a tiny boost from catching a glimpse of a hawk while I was on a bike ride, partly because, hey, it's a hawk, but mostly because I knew I could add "hawk" to my list of wildlife. Pretty soon, I could see the potential to track all kinds of things while in transit: male versus female exercisers, or number and type of discarded beverage containers. Humans are natural observers of patterns. We enjoy repetition and ritual and continuity. Beyond being driven to track by the relentless movement of the clock and the electronic calendar, we enjoy the persistence of ourselves over time.

Self-tracking is also revelatory, and consequently, for some of us at least, motivating. It seems like a logical means to accomplish change, complete tasks, and meet goals. Feedback is an important part of the motivation to stick to one's goals and projects, as Ben Franklin's regular study of his moral improvement booklet would suggest. As I walk around with a pedometer on me at all times, seeing the record of my footsteps accumulate encourages me to do more. So much the better if I can cross-check that information with the number of kilometres I've walked and the number of calories (distressingly few, actually) that rack up from walking thousands and thousands of steps. The kid inside us who likes to get the gold star will work to see those steps build up to meet the goal.

In his book *The Decision Tree*, about the coming age of personalized medicine, Thomas Goetz, a journalist and executive editor of *Wired* magazine, documents considerable evidence that test subjects will often perform better, or be more compliant, when they are aware of participating in a study (the so-called Hawthorne Effect).[10] He also points to evidence, through studying the success of weight-loss programs such as Weight Watchers, that behaviour change is easier when people engage in regular tracking of goals, get feedback on those goals, and – significantly for our purposes – can distill those goals into something like a numerical target.[11] This setting of reachable steps or goals for behaviour change isn't just the product of our numerically focused age. Lejeune offers the example of religious journals kept by some nineteenth-century girls, which were

> laid out in columns like account books. They used one page for each week and one line for each day with two columns, one marked "V" for victories (over the Devil) and the other marked "D" for defeats, with the total at the bottom.[12]

The reduction of personality change and moral rectitude to a ledger sheet may seem a little silly, but that desire for a neat accounting is surely something we share with those journal-keeping gals.

Beyond the straightforward desire for change, however, what we are often looking for in self-tracking is a tool for increased self-understanding and insight. It's through observing the "data self" that this monitoring creates that we see a portrait of who we are over time. It *seems*, at least, to be a more accurate picture of who we "really" are, rather than who we would like to perceive ourselves as being. Remember Nicholas Felton, our information designer and self-tracker extraordinaire? The first time I interviewed him, which was for my CBC radio show, *Spark*, I specifically asked him if his tracking had led to a change in his behaviour. He acknowledged that when he looked back at what he'd done during the year, it inevitably gave him incentive to try to improve his behaviour in some areas. This wasn't the *reason* for self-tracking though. His motivation came more from the revelatory character of the data. As he said of the various self-tracking projects he's created:

> while they may not be vastly interesting when I create them, they get more and more interesting as every year passes. So the time-lapse video that I did of one day in my first job was semi-interesting then, and now it's fascinating ten years later to look at myself as a young man entering profes-sional life . . .

I don't think he's alone in this, enjoying the insight gained in seeing yourself at some remove, over time. In some ways, that insight is accompanied by an almost uncanny feeling, seeing yourself *outside* yourself, as it were. Perhaps it's akin to looking back at an adolescent diary from the perspective of adulthood. The self-reportage is yours, you know you wrote it, and yet the you that is on the page – that proto-adult writing herself into being – seems unfamiliar, perhaps even unrecognizable. For some people, such as Felton, the attraction is also artistic, and perhaps even philosophical. There is pleasure to be had in data; it's the pleasure we take in patterns, an almost aesthetic experience. Perhaps it's that as humans we have a collective predisposition toward what's called *apophenia*, a tendency to see patterns in random data. The pattern of our data seems to carry an explanatory power, a sense that life isn't random or arbitrary, that, over time, the trivial acts of our mundane daily life shape a picture of who we are. We see our data bloom into patterns like a kind of emergent intelligence, becoming a self-generated portrait.

## SELF-GOVERNMENT:
## THE MODERN PROJECT AND THE PRODUCTIVE SELF

It turns out, then, that self-tracking isn't a zany invention of digital culture. Its roots reach back into our collective history, both technological and cultural, and in the very idea of modern identity. I mean modern here in its political/ philosophical sense – the economy, culture, and sense of self that emerged from the seventeenth century.

The eminent Canadian philosopher Charles Taylor has used the term "the punctual self" to describe this sense of the self, which, he says, came into its own with the philosophy of John Locke in the latter part of the seventeenth century. As Taylor describes it, it's the rise of a notion of the individual who makes a reflexive turn toward self-examination. It's the rise of a "disengaged" subject. "Disengagement," he writes, "demands that we stop simply living within the body or within our traditions or habits and, by making them objects for us, subject them to radical scrutiny and remaking."[13] It's not simply that, as the history of society and economics clearly shows, we have become a society oriented to the individual; it's also that a certain idea of what it is to be a self – a disciplined subject driven to self-control – has been installed as a core part of the culture. As Taylor puts it "the tremendous strength of Locke's punctual self through the Enlightenment and beyond comes also from the central place of the disengaged, disciplinary stance to the self in our culture."[14] This disengaged subject describes the sense of self and identity that supports self-tracking. The punctual self, as Taylor has it, is a self that is ready to apply instrumental rationality to the goal of mastering the self. When examined in this context, self-tracking is of a piece with the modern history of applying techniques to ourselves, procedures that are designed to craft a vision of the body, and of the self. It is part of the modern project to submit the self to study, to make the self a site of observation and scrutiny, but also to submit oneself to technology in order to meet a performative ideal. Seeing the self this way is bound up with the project of modernity, but it is undoubtedly more fully formed now. Our sense of ourselves as technologized bodies that we can shape and produce is now more than ever a part of our scientized, technologized, medicalized culture. Self-tracking really only makes sense as a full-flight cultural phenomenon when we think of ourselves in this way.

Julie Rak, the diary expert from the University of Alberta, pointed out to me the connection between self-tracking and philosopher and historian Michel Foucault's ideas of "governmentality," the processes by which we are produced as governable subjects. Foucault famously used the concept of Jeremy Bentham's Panopticon as a sort of master metaphor for how we came to internalize a sense of self-regulation. The Panopticon was a model of prison design. Prison cells would be positioned around a central tower from which the guard could see the cells. However, the prisoners would never know if they were being watched or not. Consequently, the idea was that prisoners would always behave. They would become self-regulating, self-monitoring individuals. Foucault links this image of the Panopticon to the set of disciplinary practices that arose historically alongside Taylor's "punctual self," shaping the modern identity into a self-disciplined, productive, conforming body. Seen in this way, self-tracking, assisted by our contemporary tools, is an extension of that Panopticon-like, internalized gaze. In fact, as we adopt these intimate tools of self-scrutiny and record-keeping, the technology works us over as never before.

Inevitably, outside expectations and norms about regulation and performance influence personal tracking – we need only look at an earlier era's devotion to the clock as a way of producing productive bodies ready for the discipline of industrializing, urbanizing society. In our own lives now, where is the line between establishing and self-administering an exercise routine because you want to do so, and doing so because you are conforming to an ideal of public health and external norms of sexual attractiveness? It's clear that self-tracking is woven through with the kinds of expectations and internalized norms Foucault wrote about. I think this is part of the picture that explains self-tracking as of a piece with the modern, Western project. It does, though, leave some things out of count.

Self-tracking is also a way of "documenting the self into being." A typical teenager writes her thoughts in her private diaries and re-reads them later, as a way of seeing how her emotional life has changed. As we grow into adulthood, looking back over that record of our emotional states is a way to understand our emotions, to *write* the self into being, at a time when our adult emotional lives and values are just being formed. When we are young, we track our shifting states of being precisely because they feel so precarious. Beyond ideas of "self-improvement" or productivity, self-tracking is an effort at finding the self through the act of documentation. It is a way of creating and reinforcing a self that has substance, a history, and, most importantly, physicality. That is, as I make myself into an object of inquiry and record my observations, I am tethering the self, grounding it, making it real, and persistent. It is a thing that I can point to, and point *others* to.

This desire to, in effect, *create* the self, by documenting the self and turning it into a site of observation, is not new. For the first time, though, it's easy to share this tracking widely with others. We can create an online mirror of our flesh-and-blood selves, linked to real, physical locations and shared widely with those around us. For the first time in our long history of documenting and self-monitoring, we are truly able to create public and constantly updated Data Maps of ourselves. What, after all, would be a better expression of the known, articulated, studied body than a Data Map that shows objectively tabulated information about the otherwise fragile, elusive idea we call the self?

As moderns, we share with Ben Franklin that goal of creating a perfectible, scrutinized self. The power in that is behaviour change. Used appropriatedly, as Quantified Self-er, Carlos Rizo, described it, it's a tool for checking in on, and tuning in to, the self. The risk, though, is that we objectify the body, and thereby make a thing of ourselves.

Our desire to self-track is in keeping with the modern idea of the self, and yet I think this digital, statistical self is also something new. It is more objectified, and also more externalized. Fundamentally, being a digital, self-tracking self is about pushing oneself out into the world, about using that ability to publish and share, to extend the self. The challenge, for this new, digital self, is not to lose touch with interiority, with introspection, and with intimate communion with the body.

# THREE

# THOROUGHLY MODERN SELF-TRACKING

*Radically Shareable, Rearrangeable, Location-Specific Monitoring*

I suppose you could think of those seventh-century monks, their tablets attached to their waists, as proto-tweeters, clattering down the hallways of the monastery carrying status updates about their thoughts with them, ready to share with the abbot. In spite of its deep cultural roots, though, today's self-tracking is a whole new ball game. Our relationship to data has changed dramatically, and self-tracking has gone from being an individual, personal practice, shared only with confidants, to being one that is radically social. More than that, this newly public information can be moved: rearranged, aggregated, sliced, and diced. This public data – and this is truly new – is increasingly linked to real, physical locations. Our forebears might have had ad hoc records that they could choose to share with people they knew. We now have a Data Map: a digital copy of our real-world activity. It is powerful, scary, enlightening, and weird in equal measure.

## SHARE AND SHARE ALIKE

Recall Nicholas Felton, the information designer who publishes *The Feltron Annual Report*, his yearly recounting of the details of his life? If his *Reports* are a path to self-knowledge and insight, they have been inherently limited by being about his solitary, direct experience of the world around him, while life is inherently social. Back in 2009, Nicholas decided to do something to address that. Instead of tracking his solitary behaviours, he decided to log data about his relationships with other people. He took note of everyone with whom he had what he calls a "meaningful encounter." He then asked all those people to complete an online survey about their experience with him: their prevailing mood, the food they consumed, whether and where they travelled during their encounter, and so forth. As he describes the project on his website:

> From parents to old friends, to people I met for the first time, to my dentist . . . any time I felt that someone had discerned enough of my personality and activities, they were given a card with a URL and unique number to record their experience.

Amazingly, he had a 32 per cent response rate. Leaving 68 per cent of his social interactions undocumented certainly skews the results, but nonetheless he's created a fascinating snapshot of his social relationships over the course of a year. Visitors to the site can see the movements and behaviours not just of Nicholas but of the people he encountered during that time.

I called up Nicholas in July of 2010 to get an update on this new chapter in self-tracking. I was curious about how the people he met reacted:

> Well, if they knew my work, they were pretty excited in general, and if they didn't know it, it was a little awkward for both of us, I think, because they were being asked to do me a favour, and I' was potentially revealing one of the odder things that I do to someone I didn't know very well.

I was surprised, initially, that so many people would go to the website and fill in information for Nicholas's project. I shouldn't have been. Humans are almost compulsively social creatures, after all, and we will use whatever tools are at our disposal to break out of our solitude and share the narratives of our lives. What's different today is that we have the tools to share that information easily – almost carelessly – and statistical data is a big part of the way we tell our stories now. Nicholas's project may be on the extreme end of opening up one's record-keeping to others, but as soon as digital technology made it easy to capture personal data, upload it, and make it both public and shareable, we wanted in.

The blossoming of what's come to be known by the shopworn but handy shorthand Web 2.0 (meaning the way that websites are used as platforms for people to upload and interact with information online) has provided much of the technological fuel for today's distinctively social, shared form of self-tracking. It also makes it easier for users to interact with others online. For comparison's sake, suppose that in the 1.0 vision of the Web I run a website about weight loss, which I can add information to and you can read. In the Web 2.0 vision, you and I can both maintain profiles and upload information to, say, Weightloss.com, and we can interact with each other's data. Facebook, Flickr, Twitter, Wikipedia, all our social media, are examples of this more interactive, dynamic, Web 2.0 world. Partly, our new, Web 2.0 world fosters our new, public self-tracking for purely technical reasons: it's literally easier to put information online and share it. But it also marks a change in values. As Gary Wolf has pointed out,[1] social media has made us comfortable being public with personal information, akin, I would say, to the way the cellphone has taken what used to be private and made it public. We simply assume (maybe incorrectly) that what we share is of interest to those we choose to share it with, and a matter of indifference to those we don't.

Add to those Web 2.0 technologies the boom in purpose-built mobile devices for tracking, and in cellphones kitted out not only with GPS and accelerometers, so they can measure direction and movement, and the pieces are in place for the culture of continual, shareable self-tracking. In 2010, the number of cellphone subscribers worldwide topped five billion, according to BBC News, with phones increasingly commonplace in the developing world.[2] Even granting that many of those aren't "smart" phones, the fact that billions of people are walking around with tiny computers in their pockets will play a huge role in the way this easy self-tracking transforms our world.

So, it's easy; it's also, well, cool. Easy-to-use online software means you don't have to be a designer, or even mathematically inclined, to turn those stats into gorgeous, professional-looking graphics and sophisticated analytics. When I used RescueTime to monitor my computer use, it delivered a weekly email analytics report, breaking down exactly how I had spent my time the previous week, grouping the types of websites I'd visited. These are metrics that, in a previous era, only large businesses with an efficiency expert and an overzealous interest in employee productivity might have had. Now, though, we have become the efficiency experts of our own lives.

That whiz-bang technology fuels our desire to share the ordinary details of our lives isn't surprising; an earlier generation had to put up with hours-long slide shows of the neighbours' trip to the Rockies, after all. What's startling is that there's such a lively interest in tracking other people's self-tracking. Online sharing makes it easy to build communities of interest, with friends or strangers, around shared hobbies, for example. Twenty years ago, I could have published a flyer listing all of my bicycle rides over the course of a year, but it's hard to imagine anyone wanting to look at it. It's only with the tools of Web 2.0 that personal data-sharing becomes both realistic and desirable. I wouldn't have much luck giving away my paper flyer on a street corner, because I would have no way of targeting avid cyclists looking for new bike routes, but no such concerns exist in an information-rich online environment where one can find everything and anything, and which caters to every niche interest.

People who share similar health concerns, for example, can share information, tips, and symptoms at a site such as CureTogether.com. If you are mapping information about your runs using your Nike+ or another system, why not make it shareable with people who enjoy the same sorts of routes as you do? In addition to finding like-minded people, if you're trying to accomplish a goal, making information public and social can be motivating, so there is a practical incentive not only to upload your own data but also to be interested in other people's. Carlos Rizo, the Quantified Self-er, sees the sharing and collaboration of today's movement as a natural outgrowth of self-tracking. As he says of sites that help people who are healing or dealing with medical conditions, "patients talk openly about what's going on with their lives, what treatments they're getting . . . they share notes . . . the community starts watching out for one another, 'hey, did you take your medication today?' . . ." He tells me there are even cases where groups of people with the same medical condition will band together to approach doctors, as a way of empowering themselves and getting better information and optimal care.

Even with more banal self-help projects, sharing can be important. B. J. Fogg, our human-computer interaction specialist, told me he thinks the ability to share our goals gives extra oomph to behaviour change. Our ability to share personal data allows for social rewards:

Some rewards aren't very enduring, you get tired of them . . . but I think the way we are psychologically, as social creatures, being admired by others, getting attention from others, getting feedback from others, those things are endlessly rewarding.

As an example of this social reward system, Fogg points to a website created by one of his former students. Goal Mafia (tag line: "Execute your goals") encourages a social networking approach to goal achievement. Members set a goal and invite friends to join their "mafia." Through a game-like combination of carrots and sticks, people are motivated to stick to their goals more than if they were just pursuing rewards privately. (Not everyone agrees that sharing our goals is the key to reaching them, however. There's some evidence that when we talk about our goals, we've subconsciously convinced ourselves we're doing something about getting there, making it less likely that we'll actually take the necessary steps.[3])

## I LIKE YOU, BUT NOT IN THAT WAY

This public sharing of our activities extends beyond the narrow bounds of physical self-improvement, though, to the continual registering of attitudes, tastes, and whereabouts, which I'm calling auto-reportage. It's like a perpetual ECG readout of states of mind, attitudes, and favourites. A perfect example of how that perpetual documentation is becoming the norm is the tyranny of the Like button. To be online now, through social media, is to submit to a nearly continuous survey about your likes, tastes, and preferences. The Web today is the social Web, and it's constantly taking its own temperature. Even if you don't consciously set out to track what you're doing, the current structure of many social networking sites provides the incentive and means to start. This is most obvious to users of Facebook, who go about their Facebook lives "liking" things, and listing preferences. Someone posts a status update about his trip, and several of his friends "like" it. We can get a better sense of who someone is by seeing what they have said they enjoy: the television shows, causes, and projects that define them. Increasingly, the listing of preferences through "liking" spills out to the broader Web. If, for example, I log in with Facebook while I visit the *New York Times* website, I will see what stories my friends commented on and liked. As the practice of liking extends beyond social-networking sites themselves to the Web more generally, we get used to this public reporting of tastes and values as an inevitable part of being online.

I don't "like" things as a rule, but even if it is not my inclination to spread my likes across the Web as though I were sowing seeds in a farmer's field, because this constant reportage is part of the currency of the Web, it's easy to experience a sort of coercive "liking." For instance, a friend of mine, who is both a fine musician and a fine friend, was organizing the necessary social-media military campaign that's become *de rigueur* for pop musicians in the twenty-first century. When her music was picked up for airplay by an online radio station, being added to the playlist came with instructions encouraging her to let everyone in her circle of fans know about it, and to get them to click "like," beside her song, live, when it was on-air. Clearly, the station wasn't interested simply in polling. They were interested in attracting more listeners by exposing them to programming by similar artists, which would play as we waited for the four-minute window during which we could say we "liked" our artist.

This move toward constant checking in and status updates, isn't happening just because humans like to share. As in the case of the Internet radio station, it arises because there are sound business reasons for it. Yes, sharing is the point of social networking, but it's also the point of the *business* of social networking. The more we define and report on our tastes, movements, and preferences, the more we participate in the social barometer of liking things, the more targeted a market we are for advertising, and for marketing to our friends. Continually pumping out and externalizing our tastes and preferences, which is so much a part of what it's like to be a digital person right now, is not just spontaneous. It's engineered. More than that, though, the bias of the technology, itself, encourages this same tendency to push data about ourselves out into the world. Digital technology "likes" itemized lists that can be moved from one context and put into another, collated with people who like the same things as we do. All the better to see you with, my dear.

Beyond the business case, there's a useful social function to all our status updates and likes as well. Technology writer Clive Thompson has talked about social-media status updates as a kind of "ambient awareness." We are passively, peripherally aware of what our friends and acquaintances are up to, but only occasionally do we actually hone in on that information and actively respond to it.[4] It's a way of "being in touch," he writes, in the same sort of way that being in a room with someone makes you aware of them. The difference, of course, is that the ambient awareness I have of a friend when we're both in a room reading the paper doesn't need to be made explicit; I know how my friend feels by body language, by physical presence. In our new, digital lives, though, ambient awareness is achieved precisely by making explicit statements about how we are feeling and what we are doing. The digital realm requires replacing that which is embodied and physical with that which is literal, specific, and disembodied.

We also share this specific subset of self-tracking (tastes, preferences, and activities) simply to apply a social filter to the massive amounts of information we have online today. These tools help us get to the heart of what we're interested in faster, by letting us know what like-minded people think, like, and do, whether that's because they're our actual friends or simply people who seem to have the same taste as we do. Self-tracking that is about purchases, or tastes, can serve this social search function nicely. Those banal status updates, or "check-ins" at particular locations, are not just going out into the ether, or helping you become "mayor" of a place, they're helping to create a useful cloud of information resources for the people you're connected to. If you check in to the same burrito place and the same bakery as Simone, but she goes to a different Indian restaurant, well, maybe she knows something you don't. If Marshall is listing all of the music he's listening to on a music-sharing site, and I am connected to him because we have similar taste in R&B, I may want to know that he just bought the new Janelle Monáe album.

The great advantage of this sharing is that it greatly expands my social and informational connections without much effort. I don't need to be in the same city with my pals, let alone the same room, to have "ambient awareness" of how they're doing, and to know whether I need to follow up with the one who just changed her relationship status to single and said she likes ice cream and double chocolate brownies. I can learn an enormous amount about what's new, helpful, and of personal interest to me from the loose ties I have in these shared social and informational spaces. Casual, online social sharing comes at the cost of depth and intentionality, of course. Casually learning about new music is different from a friend crafting a "mix tape" specifically for you. The beauty of it is that we can learn about people we can't be physically near. The danger is that we lose touch with the subtleties of the embodied presence of those we care for. I don't mean that we will stop enjoying being physically with others, but that we may undervalue the role of ongoing physical presence of others in our self-discovery.

For practical, interpersonal, and business reasons, then, we are moving self-tracking way beyond the scope of previous generations into continual sharing of our self-tracking. And with the rise of these practices, we are moving into a different self-understanding. This sharing self is often dismissed as narcissistic, but I don't think that's it at all. This self that ticks off what it likes, where it's going, how it feels, and shares this with others, is a self that is driven to reach out and present a digital *picture* of itself. As in the case of Ben Franklin, the modern self has long been interested in personal documentation and accounting, but today's tracking involves pushing the "I" out into digital space, extending it. It is a more connected and social self, but it is also more externalized and objectified, an image of self that we can point to and say, "There, that is me."

## DEEPER REASONS FOR SHARING:
## THE COLLECTIVE PSYCHE

Beyond the practical benefits, sharing helps us learn not just about individuals, but about people generally, and this too, has deep effects on our self-understanding. For the first time, we can actually have Thompson's "ambient awareness" not only of our friends, but also of the broader online community. Anyone who spends a lot of time online, on the social Web, can tell you about the moments of insight – and even awe – that come from witnessing this new sharing in action. It can give you a sense of the human condition in the early twenty-first century. It's why group movements spread so quickly online, because you can so much more readily identify with the collective. While the digital can weaken the one-to-one intimacy of analog, it strengthens our connection to the broader whole.

The rise of social-media tools have shown me something about myself: I like to watch. When you visit Nicholas Felton's site, Daytum.com, you can see the recent updates of the other users of the service, much like a Facebook news feed for people you don't know. Users can easily send updates from their cellphones, so the stream of personal updates is as frequent as a user wants. I found myself interested in studying other people's profiles. Just what are these fellow self-trackers up to? One woman tracked her "irrational fears," demonstrating, I thought, a remarkable level of personal clarity. Another person monitored the characters that turn up in his dreams (I really think it's time to get beyond those college days, dude). From what I observed, an extraordinary percentage of users are interested in their beverages, in keeping with the self-tracking preference for what is objective and physical. There's one tracker, who, amongst other things, tracks emails sent and received – that is a Big Time Commitment. I don't know who these people are, of course, and it doesn't matter. In fact, it doesn't really even matter that the information is, well, overwhelmingly dull. The dreamer isn't dreaming about killing his father, the drinkers aren't tossing back 9 a.m. shots of absinthe and tequila. The quotidian – banal even – nature of the information, though, only seems to make their reportage more familiar, more universal. This may hold the key to a deep reason why we like to share our data.

Darren Barefoot, a prominent social-media figure in Canada, who describes himself as a writer, technologist, and marketer, has spoken about the nature of art, or the artistic impulse, online. What the online experience allows, he argued, is the beauty of repetition and aggregation. Because data reporting is easy, data storage is ever cheaper, and because there are just so darn many people online, the repetition of accumulated detail is a particular fascination of the Web. We can glimpse individual behaviour, but repeated again and again. This is far from the experience of reading the diary of an exceptional person, like Benjamin Franklin, which we might do in order to gain insight into his character, or in order to emulate his daily habits. It's not even about following the confessional writing of a particular blogger. This is about the experience of ordinary reality that makes us human. On the Web we often see glimpses of individual experience repeated over and over with different individuals. The interplay of an individual snapshot with collective experience, unfolding over time, can be a powerful experience. It's why watching YouTube can sometimes feel profound, in spite of the general banality of the actual content.

A terrific example of this phenomenon is the Web project We Feel Fine by Jonathan Harris and Sep Kamvar. For years, We Feel Fine has been taking the emotional pulse of the Web. The system scans for use of the words "I feel" or "I am feeling" in blog posts. It then reprints the whole sentence, along with, if available, geographical and other information about the poster. You launch the applet, and see dozens of brightly coloured little dots on a black background. Each of those dots represents a blog entry. Hovering over one, you can see the emotion: "bad," "obsessed," whatever. Click on one of the dots and you see the full blog sentence. They can range from the perplexing ("i still feel that goat love is doing all those things but it has also become a place for me to experiment with my writing") to the touching ("I have been a bit distracted with bella the last two years so sometimes I feel like I have missed out on things with max but I have made a strong resolution that it stops now") to the eye-rolling ("i still have no feeling in my stomach from my tummy tuck so I knew the piercing wouldn't hurt"). There are quite touching examples of the intensity of some people's emotions (someone worrying about anorexia on the day I looked), but because they are just glimpses of people you will never know, you view even intense emotions at a distance, more akin to something you might read in fiction and be touched by.

Whether it's at We Feel Fine, or Daytum, or any number of sites where we can dip our toes in the water of collective daily experience, curiously, it's the lack of depth or context that ultimately offers insight. This being the Internet and all, you can do a blog search of the various phrases and find the blogs they came from. The tummy-tuck person appears to be a woman who has lost seventy pounds. The piercing was a reward for losing that first fifty pounds, which of course puts a whole different light on the tummy tuck and the piercing. The real pleasure and insight, though, comes not from deeply exploring an individual, of seeing who the people are (or claim to be). It's the iteration of everyday sentiment, pulled out of its context and reassembled alongside others, in the way that the digital realm excels at, that makes We Feel Fine, in particular, work as art. Their joys, sorrows, rages, and everyday behaviours take on a universal quality, as natural and ubiquitous as breathing.

To me, the fascinating thing about Twitter is precisely its iterative quality. The dispersed auto-reportage of users will occasionally gel around a "trending topic" or cause, in what looks like a kind of emergent intelligence of the collective. In the past, those shared, collective experiences were reserved for times of political foment (not always for the good) or, at least, for moments of shared physical proximity. Think of people coming together to mourn the death of Diana, Princess of Wales, for instance. Now that link between the individual and the collective is no longer connected to geography. It's easy to dismiss that sense of individual experience mirrored in the group online as fleeting, or trivial, and in some ways it is, but so are most such real-world experiences, linked as they are to a response to a temporal incident and connected to a gathering in real, physical space: the crowd at a concert or a sporting event. It's ephemeral, and not very "important," except that the feeling of being lost in a crowd, of seeing yourself precisely as unexceptional, can be profound. The emotional appeal of sharing "This is where I am, this is what I'm doing right now, here's what I'm feeling at this moment" is less about the actual content of what's being shared, and more about realizing that you are not alone, that there are others like you.

## CONTEXT IS (NO LONGER) KING

The shareability of our self-tracking and auto-reportage goes hand in hand with another feature of digital technology, which is that it's particularly good at taking things from one context and putting them in another. By its very nature, of course, raw figures could be moved about and used for other purposes in an analog world, too; it's just that digital technology makes this process fantastically easy and thus practical for purposes it once wouldn't have been. Individual content, whether that's status updates, opinions, distances run, or beverages consumed, can be aggregated and used for purposes other than its original intent. That's what makes We Feel Fine so remarkably effective. The fact that we can recontextualize our self-tracking is strikingly new. Our seventh-century monks and their tablets may have been proto-tweeters, but their writing was always in context. You couldn't make a We Feel Fine collaborative map out of the content of many individuals' tablets.

An individual seeking personal insight can track lots of different types of things, collate them, and compare the results. For someone trying to change or understand her behaviour, that's a valuable tool. When we are self-tracking digitally, we are able to interact with our data and reconfigure our personal information in a way Ben Franklin couldn't. I can measure my bike riding, for instance, as manifest over time, but I can also take that same data and correlate it with, say, the weather, or my weight. The ability to reassemble information in new ways makes personal metrics much more powerful, allowing us to understand the meaning of our behaviour in a new way. For some self-trackers, this means they can create a sort of personal lab for themselves, conducting experiments in productivity or behaviour change, figuring out what works, and which variables shape activity. Recontextualizing information works particularly well when sharing self-tracking. You could have a music service that lists my preferred music genres, for instance. That could be collated with the profiles of others so that a new list turns up people who like both country and hip hop, or people who like country and hip hop but don't like June Carter or Jay-Z. A person with a medical condition might want to look at other people's profiles based on the severity of certain shared symptoms one day, and by length of illness the next.

The real power in the way digital technology allows for the recontextualization of data comes at the macro level. We're seeing the proliferation of tools that do just this. There are tools to perform what's called sentiment analysis on Twitter: all tweets about a product name or a political leader, for example, can be grouped together and scanned for the prevailing sentiment attached to it. Historically, self-tracking was connected with the person in his totality; now, that data can float free, unmoored. And it can be used in any number of ways.

## LOCATION, LOCATION, LOCATION

The final, new piece of the puzzle in twenty-first-century self-tracking is the way it is increasingly connected to real, physical locations. Ben Franklin may have kept a meticulous record, documenting his flaws and failings, but his information was not in *its essence* linked to a particular geography. Today, though, our self-monitoring is increasingly connected to real, physical places. There's no reason why a self-tracker twenty, or two hundred, years ago might not have added details about where she was when a particular event occurred; what's different now is that our data can be *inherently* linked to location. Now that we have GPS-enabled phones and other devices, reporting on a behaviour includes the ability to tag it with location-based information. For instance, let's say you love to hike. Why not sign up to be a member at EveryTrail.com? Create a profile of yourself, indicating your preferred activities, download the app for your GPS-enabled smart phone, and start tracking your hiking. As you move, the GPS-enabled device "knows" where you're going. You needn't have your orienteering badge to link what you did to where you went. You'll see a map of, say, the Humber River valley trail in Toronto, and your path along it marked in red, and annotated by any photos you took along the way. You can push out your trail information to people who are friends or followers on Twitter or Facebook. Remember what I said about how much we like to share? Disregard it in this case. Trust me, no one you know on Facebook wants to look at a map of where you went hiking. The people who probably do want to see that information, though, are the hiking enthusiasts you can link up with through the social-networking component of EveryTrail.com. This is contemporary self-tracking in action. What was once a personal experience of going for a walk through the Humber River trail, perhaps to be recorded in your daily diary, or in a little list of memorable hikes, has become an annotated, shared, location-aware experience.

So casual is it to do something like check in with a location-based service such as Foursquare, we don't think about how odd it is that our location is known and shareable, with minimal effort on our part. Beyond listing our behaviours and tastes, we continually update where we were physically when those behaviours occurred. We are becoming creatures who continually plot ourselves on maps, in everything from check-ins to Google Street View. Julie Rak, the University of Alberta academic who studies the history of diaries, spoke about the significance of this location-based shift in self-tracking:

> It is now possible with a computer to do what only high level intelligence services have been able to do, which is pinpoint your own exact location in relation to other things and know where other people are exactly. That's a spy thing and now anyone can do it. So to me, that changes our understanding of our relationship to the world we're in, our relationship to our country, and it shrinks the world in a way that even travel doesn't do.

With the addition of location-based information, we are turning our direct experience not just into data but into an actual map, a graphical representation of our actions and experiences. The impulse to self-track, as we've seen, comes out of the desire to make the self into a site of study. As Rak points out, the ability to create an objective map of ourselves changes our understanding of our relationship to the world around us. The simple act of going for a hike has been altered, and provides a further example of the link between contemporary self-tracking and a shift in the way we understand ourselves. It's no longer about the subjective, experiential domain of feeling ourselves in our bodies in nature. It is a deeply mediated and objectified experience.

## WHEN SELF-TRACKING MEETS THE GEOWEB

When the information we're putting out there is tagged with geographic data, we're contributing to what's called the Geoweb (or geospatial web). With these tags, the information online isn't just searchable by topic, but by location.

To use a commonplace example, the fact that photographs taken with many cellphone cameras can be tagged with location means that they can be associated with a place. Online maps often contain photos that have been previously tagged with this information, or have been simply been plotted on the map. That's an example of the Geoweb in action. Taken to its extreme edge, you can imagine it as an enormous online mirror of the physical world around you. As we start to connect our self-tracking and auto-reporting with location, we contribute to that Geoweb. By posting geotagged photos or mapping our hikes, we are collectively creating maps of location-based information. This means that the more location-tagged, shareable, information we put out there, the more complete the searchable online equivalent becomes.

One example of the intersection of self-tracking and the Geoweb is the restaurant review website Urbanspoon.com, which brings together newspaper reviews, blog posts, and user ratings of restaurants. At random, I picked out one user, "Jen," and checked out her profile. She's a self-described "foodie" and her profile lists lots of the sorts of fun self-tracking data a foodie might be interested in. It not only lists Jen's pocket reviews, and what she likes and dis-likes, it breaks down personal metrics for her, such as the

is so large and much more mainstream than the geek-chic Foursquare.

As I write this, it's too early to say whether locati[on] sharing will take off as a mainstream activity in the wa[y] social networking has. According to research from[...] Internet and American Life research body, in a stu[dy] late in 2010, just 4 per cent of online adults [...] services like Foursquare,5 but of course, on[...] working was once a fringe activity too. To[...] of location-based check-ins is in equal [...] creepy. The potential for inadverten[...] with the wrong people is worrisome, esp[...] social-network friendships are leaky around the e[...]

Some of the inevitable privacy concerns about sha[...] location data came up in 2010, when some Dutch web designers launched PleaseRobMe.com. Their satirical point was simply to draw attention to the potential implications of broadcasting to the world where you are. Some people who check in on Foursquare choose to send their updates not only to their immediate circle of friends but also to push that information out on the public timeline on Twitter. All the designers of PleaseRobMe.com did was bring that publicly available information together in one place. The idea was simply to show that when you're publishing where you are, you're also publishing the fact that you're not home. Now, there are lots of reasons why you might not take this terribly seriously as a problem: who is to say there's no one else at home? Is there really much evidence that burglars are actively trolling social media trying to figure out who is where? But the point is that we are rushing headlong into percentage of Japanese ... those she visited and the part... Urbanspoon can break down the ... because the restaurants are linked to real loc... power of that location-based information comes... completely unrelated person, me, say, finds hers... downtown Oakville, a city near my hometown of Toronto ... that I don't really know, I check the Urbanspoon app on my... phone. I search by type of cuisine in Oakville, and find that... Celadon House has good reviews, including Jen's. Jen is... tracking what restaurants she visited and her reactions to... them for reasons understood by her alone, but when that... data is public, searchable, and linked to real geographical... locations, it becomes useful, not just to Jen, but to anyone... who shares Jen's interests.

People are increasingly willing to link their movements... and preferences to locations in real time. What once seemed... like a very fringe activity, when early adopters used a ser-... vice like Dodgeball to text their location to groups of... friends, has bloomed into a full-blown phenomenon, with... the success of Foursquare, and other services that let... people easily check in to locations. Facebook saw the... potential power of these tools when it launched Facebook... Places in 2010, a Foursquare-esque service that allowed you... to share your location from your phone with people in your... social network. About a year later, they retired the project... but added features that allow users to indicate their loca-... tions. Location-based reporting on Facebook is the litmus... test for how far people will comfortably go with sharing... real-time self-tracking information, simply because Facebook

---

public self-monitoring without giving a lot of thought to the practical, let alone philosophical, implications of all this location-based activity. The use of any communications technology involves complex and mostly tacit social rules, and there's been very little discussion about what the proper sphere of sharing is, or whether your sense of how and what to share is the same as mine. As we become more comfortable passively sharing information about behaviour and location, we're going to have to juggle when information sharing is useful, and when it's just plain stupid.

## THE RISE OF THE PERSONAL DATA MAP

While we have long subjected ourselves to the by turns pleasurable and masochistic tracking of our daily activities, health, and frame of mind, powerful new factors – the ability to share this information easily and widely, to move it and reassemble it, and to link this digital information to real physical locations – are coming into play. This is a watershed change. It creates a Data Map, a digital version of our earthly selves. Think of this digital self as a doppelgänger, a companion, in your everyday existence. It is the sum of all those status updates about how you are feeling, what you did, how you moved, where you ate, how long you spent reading PerezHilton.com compared to *The New Yorker* online. It will often be linked to actual, physical locations, and it will often be public. What will that data-mapped self look like, as we learn to view it over time, graph it, compare it year on year, as an accountant might compare our tax picture over time? It will only get easier and more commonplace to capture all of that information seamlessly. The more we use digital tools, the more our bodies and behaviours can be displayed and described as zeros and ones. And of course, it's not just my map or your map; there are all those other data-mapped bodies out there. What can we know about ourselves as a collectivity based on all those data trails?

When Nicholas Felton asked individuals to participate in his 2009 project, he was essentially asking them to make what's really an analog effort, to remember and come to some conclusions about their interaction with him, and to document it. It's a project he could have tackled fifty years ago, albeit with a tremendous amount of effort. One can imagine a future though, where one's data streams intersect with other people's data streams in a more automatic fashion. Why not get a more complete picture of our data set by seeing how it interacts with other people in our lives? As we'll see, the power of the Data Map is not just in learning more about ourselves individually but about the broader social world we share with other people.

Humans beings create narratives about who we are in order to communicate to ourselves, and to others, what matters to us. It is possible that the data-mapped, virtual self offers a more accurate picture of who we really are than the subjective stories we tell. Maybe just as our best friends love us in spite of the manifest contradictions and falseness of those narratives, we can learn to love the data-mapped self that reveals our real behaviours, in all their complex, contra-dictory, hypocritical glory. As with all things that we track digitally, though, the data-mapped self captures best what computers do best: the literal, the specific, the objectively measurable. Our self-tracking is really about data, and number-crunching, not about exploring the intimacies of subjective experience. It conforms to the bias of digital technology, which favours this kind of on/off, yes/no, "zeros and ones" clarity and definition. And it leaves the rest out of count.

Welcome to your new digital self.

# FOUR

# THE DELIGHTS AND DAMAGE OF DIGITAL LIFE

### Self-Tracking as a Response to Losing the Ground Beneath Our Feet

M uch has been written about the impact of new, digital technology on the mind; we study cognition and attention, scanning fMRIs, looking for evidence that our love of the digital is expanding our minds or, conversely, killing our ability to focus. We think about how digital technology affects social relationships, privacy, and commerce. We don't, however, spend much time thinking about how new technology affects our bodies on an intimate level, so intimate that it changes the way we know ourselves and perceive the world around us. We don't think about it, because we are inheritors of that "punctual," highly individualized self, and view technology as a neutral tool that we can use to control what is around us.

We've seen that, in some ways, self-tracking is an extension of the broader project of "making" the modern self. We use digital technology, in particular self-tracking and auto-reportage, as a way of shoring up identity, of pushing a firm, persistent, individual self out into the virtual world. But I want to argue that digital culture also brings with it an entirely new impact on the body, one that is radically reshaping our sense of self. It's in the nature of digital technology that it disembodies us. Today's urge to document the self is an attempt not just to assert the self but also to ground the self, to tether it, to re-embody it, to give it heft and substance. Self-tracking is an adaptive reaction to the pathologies of disembodiment that are part of digital culture. The core irony of this is that the persistent, documented individual self we're trying to assert is itself an illusion. The key to repairing this illusion is the body, the very thing digital culture denies us.

## DISEMBODIMENT AND DIGITAL CULTURE

I'm not a technological determinist; I don't believe new technologies make us behave in particular ways, or change society in a predetermined sense. Technology is a form of culture, a social practice, and so new technologies are already culturally informed from the get-go. They don't arrive in our midst as neutral tools. They are political, in a sense, because they are born in a social and cultural context. In fact, the main reason I wanted to write this book is that we have the power to shape the character of our technologies, particularly in the early going, and we are at this point with technologies of self-tracking. In philosophy of technology circles, this stance is called *social constructivism*. That said, technologies are not infinitely malleable. As we've seen, it is in the character of digital technology to decontextualize and recontextualize, to remix and reassemble. That is the beauty of zeroes and ones. The remixable quality of digital information means that it is spreadable, fluid, and ripe for collaboration. To *be digital* is to feel a perpetual, lightweight sense of connection and energy; this is one of its many pleasures. You are swimming in a swiftly moving river. You are lightly linked to people all over the world. It is a thin, fast, evolving, highly collaborative culture. The speed and reach of networked culture is sometimes thrilling, often dizzying. If the culture of the book, as Marshall McLuhan would have it, is the culture of the individual point of view and sustained, linear thought, then the culture of the Web is highly dynamic. The single point of view, in this world, is not as powerful as the collective, collaborative experience. Twitter is this experience in microcosm. When do you say that something is "done" or "true" on Twitter? The whole point of Twitter is to be continually in process, fluid, swimming in an eternal now of updates, coalescing from time to time on trending topics, then bubbling over and breaking down again. In many ways, digital culture is imbued with a more organic feeling than the culture of the book, and yet the common knock on digital culture is that it's both solitary and slothful. Trot out the cultural clichés: bloggers envisioned as for some reason always being in their pajamas, tapping away alone, or gamers, overweight, pale, and doughy, playing online video games until all hours. The opposite is true. To be digital is to be almost compulsively connected to other people.

What digital culture is not, though, is grounded or embodied. To know the world through the Internet is to be disconnected from your body. Knowledge has been delinked from the physical.

## SELF-TRACKING AS ADAPTIVE STRATEGY

Media theorist Clay Shirky tells a great story, in a public talk called "Gin and the Cognitive Surplus,"[1] about the shock people dealt with in the early years of urbanization and the Industrial Revolution in Britain. As the way of life lurched from agrarian to industrial, the convulsions of this techno- logically driven cultural change were so extreme that they gave rise to the Gin Craze, a thirty-year period from 1720 to 1751, primarily confined to London, in which consumption of spirits tripled and gin was widely sold without licences.[2] As with most historical events, there are many factors that contributed to the Gin Craze. Shirky zeroes in on it as a way of managing the stress of social dislocation. Essentially, he argues, gin was the anaesthetic that helped the working class deal with massive change for a generation, until the culture finally began to adapt, to create norms and laws around the new mode of organization, and to start to see the real cultural benefits of urban, industrial life.

For his part, Shirky's position is that the anaesthetic of the twentieth century – the way we managed increased leisure time – was television. We dulled our senses in a TV-induced stupor to deal with the sudden extra time that stretched out before us. We are only now claiming what we can actually do with that leisure time, Shirky argues, by doing work on collaborative, Internet-based projects that we don't necessarily get paid for. We are learning to use our "cognitive surplus." I would argue, though, that we're in the Gin Craze phase of the digital revolution. If it's even partway true that the move from linear, print culture is as great a shift as the Gutenberg Revolution, as some media thinkers increasingly seem to believe, then we're in the midst of a tumultuous cultural shift. We know that entire industries are being disrupted by digital technology – witness the upheaval in the cultural industries, and the outsourcing (or in-sourcing) of work now that information can be easily moved all over the globe. We accept as a commonplace of media that print culture gave rise to a point of view and a new notion of what it means to be an individual. Yet we ignore that there's a powerful disruption going on in our own psyches, our own bodies, our own way of thinking about what it means to be an individual today. Self-tracking is our gin. It's an almost compulsive desire to document the actual states of being and physical presence, at the dawn of an era in which physically embodied ways of knowing are on the endangered species list.

## THE DISEMBODIED DIGITAL SELF

Marshall McLuhan was one of the few technology thinkers who really examined the intimate, deep impacts of technology on the body and the senses. He famously talked about media as "the extensions of man":

> The personal and social consequences of any medium – that is, of any extension of ourselves – result from the new scale that is introduced into our affairs by each extension of ourselves, or by any new technology.[3]

For McLuhan, electric media, such as the television and the then-rare computer, extended the nervous system. It's hard to believe that he wrote his classic work, *Understanding Media*, in 1964, nearly fifty years ago, because it seems to describe our own era of digital technology so well. As he wrote, we have become an organism "that now wears its brain outside its skull and its nerves outside its hide."[4] McLuhan describes the kind of numbing or amputation that we do to ourselves in order to deal with this kind of radical extension of the senses. Because the way a technology extends our senses is so different from how we naturally, physically understand the world around us, the other senses react in response and close down. If, as McLuhan suggests, the telephone is an extension of the ear, and the wheel is an extension of the foot, what we have in digital culture is a case of massive over-extension, this time of the nervous system. With "electric technology," he writes, "we have to numb our central nervous system when it is extended and exposed, or we will die. Thus the age of anxiety and of electric media is also the age of the unconscious and of apathy."[5] What an apt description of our own anxious, apathetic age, at once hyperconnected and remote. We are dispersed in space, able to send digital bits of ourselves all over the world. Our bodies are now extended – scattered, really – across innumerable devices, handhelds, phones, tablets, laptops, and desktop computers.

Digital technology unmoors us from conventional, embodied understanding of time and space. Our use of digital technology upends our conventional ideas of space and "here." As computers have become ever smaller, morphing into app-based phones and tablets, being digitally connected no longer implies sitting down in your house for long stretches. It's not that the digital life is anti-physical, in the sense of physical fitness (witness all those fitness tools and apps). It's that digital technology takes us out of being where we are. You only have to watch someone talking on a cellphone as she walks down the street to see this displacement, this disembodiment, in action. She is there but not there. You can tell by how awkwardly she moves, as anyone who has tried to navigate around someone on a phone on a busy sidewalk can attest. She's also not, obviously, physically with the person she's talking to, but in a kind of third, digital disembodied place. No wonder William Gibson put the "space" in cyberspace, to use that quaint old term. Digital technology creates this other sense of non-physical place. My Twitter followers and I share a virtual space; we're in the Twittersphere together. This is quite different from the way I feel when I'm lost in reading a book, which is a solitary, absorbed, private world.

In addition to this changed sense of space, our understanding of time is disrupted thanks to the asynchronous nature of so much of our communication. We scatter tweets or notes on friends' Facebook walls as though they were seeds, to be pecked at by birds whenever they happened by. The bodily experience of linear time dissolves in a media culture that is one of a perpetual collaborative, fluid, now-ness.

Beyond the way digital technology dislocates our sense of time and space, the experience of digital life is that it ungrounds us from our basic physical competence. Whatever skill it may take to maintain useful lists of people to follow on Twitter, or to code, or to understand your Facebook privacy settings, it's clearly not a *physical* sort of competence. That sense of physical expertise and the ability to respond physically to the environment around us with skill, is surely a core human competency – not to mention, pleasure – but it is a skill that's largely denied us in the digital realm. The philosopher of technology Albert Borgmann has written about the implications of living with "the device paradigm."[6] Borgmann wrote his best-known book, *Technology and the Character of Contemporary Life*, in 1984. He was responding to the accumulation of technological systems in our world. Borgmann compares a technology such as a wood-burning stove with a technological device such as a central heating system. The stove requires competence and attention, he argues, whereas a system or device such as central heating (or a computer, for that matter) requires no such attention. Learned physical skill is something that isn't required when we are pushing buttons and clicking mice and waiting for some mysterious process to happen on our hard drive or in the Cloud to give us the result we want. Being physically grounded, sensing the self in real physical space, is a core part of mental, physical, and spiritual health, and yet everywhere in contemporary culture that basic, grounding experience is denied us. This almost dissociative experience of being unmoored is an aspect of digital culture we seem oblivious to. We are animals, and yet we are failing to acknowledge just how vital a grounded, deep, embodied relationship to the world is to our well-being.

And so, as with any sort of cultural pathology, we respond blindly, trying to reclaim what we so desperately need but don't seem to quite recognize. The more driven side of gym culture is one such response, the desire to sculpt the body like an object. We carve out places in our lives for simple "analog" practices that ground the self in the body. We see this in the resurgence of DIY culture, from knitting clubs to hacker spaces. It's part of what's behind the kitchen-as-fetish object. Personally, I started gardening and cooking in earnest when my life became more digital, and I can tell you stories of digerati who make a point of finding a way to "work with their hands" in their spare time. Borgmann calls these sorts of activities "focal things and practices,"[7] activities such as gardening, playing music, running long distance, or preparing a shared celebratory meal. They are activities he describes as "inconspicuous, homely and dispersed."[8] They are also things and practices that are physical and sensual; they serve to bring mind and body together. "[T]he runner is mindful of the body," he writes, "because the body is intimate with the world."[9] Borgmann's 1984 book was written in a pre-digital era, as far as most of our personal experience is concerned; how much more true this seems to me now, in digital life.

I believe self-tracking is a different reaction to the disembodiment of digital life but one that springs from the same root. In self-tracking, we are literally trying to keep track of the body, to rephysicalize it, in an adaptive reaction to the ungrounding of the self in contemporary life. I want to be clear that it's not that there's something *wrong* with people who self-track or that they are any more neurotic than anyone else. Actually, the self-tracking crowd is ahead of the rest of society – classic early adopters – unsurprising, considering that they seem to be more likely to be people who inhabit digital culture deeply. It's not a coincidence that so much self-tracking is about the physical body. We're not shallower than people in Ben Franklin's time, but we are more detached from our bodies than ever before. Tracking the body, documenting where it is precisely in time and space, actually only makes sense in a culture of distracted disembodiment and bodily alienation. Had this technology existed when most of us lived in rural environments and worked on farms, you really can't imagine people tracking numbers of arm flings of chicken feed, or graphing the shovels-full of sheep manure moved onto kitchen gardens. Perhaps self-tracking centres on whatever the dominant cultural anxiety of the time is: in earlier times, that might have been the Ben Franklinesque concern for orderliness and productivity, or the fear that one might cease to be right with God. Today, it is a way of graphing the self into being. It is a way of saying: Look, I exist! Here is my body, what I consumed, how I moved my body through space and time.

### DON'T FORGET TO BREATHE

Disembodiment and ungrounding aren't just abstract concepts or ideas about what it's like to live digitally. There are actual basic, practical ways in which our use of digital technology uproots and ungrounds us, too. I had the good fortune to interview Linda Stone back in 2009, for my CBC Radio show *Spark* and followed up with her by email for this book. Linda is a high flyer in the tech world. A former senior executive with Apple and also with Microsoft, she is now a writer, a speaker, and a consultant who focuses, as it were, on attention. She has a fascinating take on the relationship between our digital devices and what I think of as our contemporary feeling of "disembodiment." Way back in 1998, before social media, smart phones, and the explosion of apps kicked our digital selves into overdrive, she coined the phrase "continuous partial attention" to describe the way the digital self goes through the world. Continuous partial attention is not quite the same as multi-tasking; we're

much more motivated by not wanting to miss anything . . . we want to be a live node on the network, we want to be in demand, we want to be part of this broader set of connections that are out there. And the unfortunate cost of that. . . . is when you're on top of everything, it's hard to get to the bottom of anything.

I love that image of being "a live node on the network." It's a feeling that, as Stone says, while exhilarating, takes us away from depth. Much of the time, unless I am deeply absorbed in an analog task such as reading a book, that task is accompanied by a perpetual sense that I ought to check my Twitter account, or have my BlackBerry nearby so that I can respond to, or look for – what, exactly? It feels like I'm always on the verge of being sucked out of the experience I'm in, the very place I'm in. This is the experience of continuous partial attention. We scan the digital horizon, perpetually on the lookout for the next hit. If the healthy self is grounded in the here and now, centred in what is actually happening, a life spent in anticipation of the next is fundamentally not a life spent grounded. The digital calls us into the now, but also into the next.

More recently, Linda Stone has been looking at the way our bodies respond when we are using digital technology. She coined the term "email apnea" to describe the pattern of our breathing as we interact with all our devices. It refers to the way we either take shallow breaths, or temporarily stop breathing, when we're in front of the multiplicity of screens we use.

I've practised yoga for more than twenty years, so I was immediately intrigued by the idea of email apnea. Breath, and control of the breath, is a core concept in yoga. Understanding how the breath responds, observing it, and sometimes guiding it are skills you spend a lot of time developing as a yoga student. Email apnea struck me as intuitively true, as something that fit with my own experience of digital devices. Stone recognized this email apnea in her own life, and set about studying it:

> I began a six-month, very informal study of observing and interviewing over two hundred people sitting at computers in cafés, in their offices, standing or sitting working on their mobile device, or watching people in front of a TV set . . . their shoulders are forward, their arms are forward, their

chest is caved in. You can't get a diaphragmatic breath when you're sitting like that. . . . With anticipation . . . humans most certainly do a sharp intake of breath . . . Between the inhaling [and] not exhaling (because of our posture), we were breath-holding. Many people think of breathing as the inhale, but the really important part of breathing is the exhale.

For Stone, this isn't just a problem because your mother always told you to sit up straight. She thinks this shallow breathing or breath-holding over time is prompting a fight-or-flight stress response:

Our bodies are preparing to run from a predator, only with email apnea we're sort of all dressed up with nowhere to go. . . . Noradrenaline, cortisol, glucose, cholesterol: All of these resources are there to help us move, not to sit hunched over a device doing our email.

Her take isn't that we need to stop using digital technology, but that we need to learn how to work differently with it:

Now, the good news on that is that our brains are very plastic and very resilient, and this can be shifted, using awareness and learning and practicing various breathing techniques that activate the "rest and digest" or the parasympathetic nervous system.

As Linda points out, exhalation is a central feature of relaxed healthy breathing. Long, slow exhalations provoke the "relaxation response." Those deep, slow breaths and long exhalations are what we need when we are anxious or stressed. The breath brings us back to ground. In an email, Linda tells me she has also been following the work of neuroscientist Stephen Porges, who suggests physical exercises beyond breathing to help bring people who suffer from a chronic fight-or-flight state back to a feeling of safety and balance. We aren't just talking philosophical niceties here. There are actual, practical, physical deficits inherent in our use of digital technologies.

Much as I love – and I do – my online life, and the immediate feeling of connectedness we get from digital info-snacks and the companionable nature of social media, the one thing it does *not* offer is ground. The challenge with this digital way of being – and what makes it relevant for exploring self-tracking – is that it prevents us from being truly *present*. When immersed in digital life, we are not present in time and space and, crucially, not present in the body. We are not *attending* to body, perception, and experience.

Personally, my own sense of the importance of this idea comes from my practice of yoga, partly as posture practice but more centrally as a philosophical and contemplative system of thought. In a yogic sense, observing the body and mental states in a non-judgemental way is a core concept in coming to a clearer understanding of self. It relies fundamentally on this sense of presence and attending. Georg Feuerstein is one of the West's leading contemporary scholars in yogic philosophy. By email, I asked him about the role that this sense of presence plays in taking us beyond a limited, "rigid" sense of self. He replied:

So, by being mindful of our body while assuming a posture, we are mindful in the present moment. We are not separated from our body. We are not divorced from our life world (German: *Lebenswelt*). We are not merely in our head. In Yoga, the idea is to do this in every life situation. Now, it is important to realize that self-observation is not the same as neurotic self-watching, which has an element of anxiety to it. True self-observation, while still of the mind, has a quality to it that points to the transcendental Self (purusha, ātman). It naturally breaks down the "rigid self."

This skill of simply being present, physically, leads to a very different sense of what it is to be a self. You're not trying to build up a "you," you're simply being, and being present. You don't need to be a yogi to experience the grounding effect of being fully, physically present. It's a feeling where mind and body connect deeply: you may have found it staring into a campfire, going for a long bike ride, or in Borgmann's long-distance run. In yoga, this is an experience that's guided by mindfulness and attention; for Borgmann, these practices ground us without our having to consciously attend to them. They share, though, the connection to the wisdom of the body. It's not an experience that can come to us in a disembodied digital state.

## HOW IRONIC

Self-tracking perhaps has emerged as a way to look for that abiding and attending, to try to find the body, as it were. There's a curious irony to this response, though. The tools for doing all this tracking – from pedometers to smart phones to social media – are part of what creates the ungrounded, distracted self. It's hard to get to ground by creating more opportunities for continuous partial attention and email apnea. When we get compulsive in our use of digital technologies (and believe me, as someone who is always verging on compulsive in my use of digital technologies, I understand this) we become ever more distanced from embodied experience. The disembodiment drives us to try to create the self, to document the self into being. It's a quixotic drive, though, in part because we are using the tools that take us out of ourselves in the first place. And that hard, objectified, documented, digitized numeric self that we're so insistent on is a false ideal anyway. Escaping from the anxiety that comes from disembodiment requires reconnecting with the body – not documenting or objectifying it, but residing with it.

When we are reasonable about our self-tracking, the practice can offer us insights. We can use it in a non-judgemental way, simply to observe behaviour, emotions, or activity over time. Or, heck, just because it's fun. Where we get into danger is when we tie ourselves to that objectified performative self, when we scrutinize ourselves like a butterfly pinned. Even if we're not neurotic in our self-watching, digital tools put us at risk of further self-objectification. Self-scrutiny goes beyond self-observation and subjects the self to the relentless, objective power of numbers. The digital, as I've said, is very good at reducing experience to discrete, moveable bits of information, but that is not the sum of our experience. We need to make space for that which cannot be statistically documented: inchoate, subjective, embodied experience.

## BREATH, BODY, AND BREAKS

In spite of these reservations, I do think we can use tools of self-tracking in a way that reconnects us to the body. Recall Carlos Rizo, our Quantified Self-er, who seems to have taken a deliberate stance on using self-tracking to become more in touch with what his body is telling him. As such, he is using the technology to reconnect with the physical. What we can learn from Carlos's practice is how to self-track but also how to be digital. We can, and should, adopt a critical, conscious stance to digital technology, even as we engage with it. It means taking our bodies seriously, as seriously as we take our minds. If there are physical consequences, as Linda Stone suggests, to the way we are using digital technology, we need to take that as seriously as we do the cognitive effects of that technology, whether that's in breathing, exercises, or in new approaches to design.

Stone certainly thinks that part of the challenge lies simply in better design. She tells me in an email that she thinks the iPad has changed people's posture for the better, and improved their breathing. If that's so, Stone's work suggests the physical response to digital life can be addressed, by a combination of design strategies, breathing, and other exercises. It may well help us address those issues, but I don't think it speaks to the full sense in which digital technology takes us out of ourselves.

I think we also need to take the body seriously as a site and source of knowledge. Knowledge doesn't live simply in data or simply in our heads. We know the world around us not by what the pedometer count says but by how it feels to be in this body right now. Being present is something a lot of us have forgotten how to do, and so we get in touch with our bodies by submitting them to the regimen of the gym, or to the cold, clean comfort of statistics, in order to get a sense of ourselves. That sense, though, is already within us; we just need to take the opportunity to listen to it. We can find some balance in our use of digital technologies, recognizing that we need to create space for embodied experience, time to attend quietly to what it feels like to be me right now. We just have to put down the iPhone long enough to do it.

# FIVE

# MEET YOUR DIGITAL DOPPELGÄNGER

*The Future of the Data-Mapped Self*

One morning, while procrastinating about writing this book, I took a look at one of my favourite "guilty pleasure" websites, the media gossip blog Gawker.com. It carried a *New York Post* story about a first-year teacher in Brooklyn, Ilene Feldman, who allegedly deliberately engineered a minor fall down the school staircase to avoid having her classroom observed after she had received a poor performance review.[1] Before resigning, she insisted the fall was an accident, although she refused to watch frame-by-frame footage of it. Yes, of course there was footage of the incident. It was recorded on the school's video camera. That footage, equally unsurprisingly, was posted on the *New York Post* website for all to see. We could do our own frame-by-frame analysis of it, judging whether we thought the fall looked legitimate or not. The story, and the video, was picked up by other news organizations, and last time I checked, you could still find the whole story online. I sure hope Ilene has been able to move on with her life, because her digital self hasn't. Welcome to the data-mapped self: documented, recorded, enumerated, and public. We are all Ilene Feldman now.

Ilene's actions were recorded by the school's security camera, captured by our surveillance society. But a culture of *self*-surveillance, where we ourselves are responsible for the data streams we generate, is rapidly evolving. So far, we've witnessed a patchwork of ways that data is collected, in a largely piecemeal – and voluntary – fashion. What will *we* look like when we are fully data-mapped, when there are more than isolated threads of data – some jogging routes here, some sleep diaries there – but a fully formed digital picture of what our lives are like, and how we are spending our time? This information offers powerful insights about our behaviour, but it also carries the threat of being used against us.

Creating a full Data Map of the self not only relies on the way we're becoming a culture of dedicated statisticians of the self. It also draws on the informational flotsam and jetsam that's generated simply by using digital tools. As we replace our analog tools with digital devices, we'll start to see a startlingly full picture of our behaviours, preferences, activities, and so on. As we stop reading paper books and start using e-books, keep electronic calendars instead of paper diaries, and have our location-aware cellphones with us at all times, we are passively generating data about our behaviour. As we look toward the future, then, we can see that a data-mapped self might be a near-complete record of what happens to us during a day, fuelled by deliberate self-tracking but also by the constant capture that digital technology makes possible. Insights about our life may be valuable to us, but they will also be valuable to others –our employers, our insurance companies. Who gets to use that data, and how?

We don't have to do much speculating about what this future Data Map might look like, either. The fact is, there are already people living a life of constant capture, where recording everything is the default and opting out is the exception. Welcome to the world of "life logging."

## MEET THE LIFE LOGGERS

If you want to get a glimpse of the bleeding edge of self-tracking, look to people who have made a choice to retain a digital copy of as much of what they come into contact with and experience as possible. These are people who have taken the choice to self-track to an extreme, fuelled by digital tools that make it possible to do this without the sort of extraordinary effort it would have taken even five or ten years ago.

C. Gordon Bell is likely the best known of these life loggers. He's a researcher with Microsoft Research and he has documented his documentation in the book *Total Recall*. He (along with co-author Jim Gemmell) recounts his project, MyLifeBits, which is, essentially, an attempt to record everything that goes on in his life.

Life-logging relies on the idea that "technology will allow us to capture everything that ever happened to us, to record every event we ever experienced and to save every bit of information we have ever touched."[2] Bell is "now paperless" and is beginning to capture not only what we're all digitizing – music, pictures, and books – but also IM transcripts, phone calls, memos, papers, and more. So, as you can imagine, that involved designing software that would make this possible. Bell altered his web browser so that it would make a copy not just of the URLs he visited, but of the content of every page itself; record all of his office phone calls; and save all his IMs and emails. He tracked where he went with a GPS. For a time, he recorded the TV shows he watched and radio programs he listened to, before deciding that material would be available on demand anyway. He even wore a doohickey called a SenseCam, developed by one of his fellow researchers.[3] The SenseCam is an automatic photo-taking device. You wear it around your neck and it periodically snaps pictures, opting to take photos when the light changes, or when it senses that someone is near you.

I can hear you asking: And why would I – why would anyone – want to do this? Essentially for the same reasons people engage in self-tracking more generally. Once you have a system for storing what you come into contact with, annotated with the proper metadata (i.e., what the information is, when and where it was recorded), your life, effectively, becomes searchable. "Productivity gains will come from understanding one's work habits better. With a detailed e-memory of what I do, my computer is my personal time management consultant."[4] Sounds like my RescueTime experiments on steroids. In addition, as Bell and Gemmell point out, human memory is fallible.[5] In fact, some of the most interesting research associated with this technology is for people with cognitive impairments. For instance, researchers at the University of Toronto's TAGlab (Technologies for Aging Gracefully) have been experimenting with using the SenseCam as a memory aide, allowing people to effortlessly record memorable events so that they can refer to them later. With our aging population, many of us fall somewhere on the grey scale of fallible memory, and besides, there's far too much media and information to remember anyway. There will likely be lots of people with an interest in simple, searchable databases of their lives.

I've been using the metaphor of a map to talk about the data we're gathering, but at least part of that information really will be a map. Much of the data you create will be tagged with metadata not only about time but also about location, since an implication of tracking all this data is that it can be linked to real physical locations. We're already doing this, of course, when we snap a photo with a location-aware camera, but as self-tracking increases, so will location-mapping. In a life-logging future, the Map of You may be searchable by location.

When I read Bell and Gemmell's book, it seemed so extreme I couldn't imagine there ever being a market for something like MyLifeBits – and indeed, the technology isn't designed to come to market; it's a research project. But I no longer think it's that extreme; I think, as do Bell and

Gemmell, that it's probably going to be mainstream to track our everyday comings and goings this way. Data storage has become so cheap that it's feasible to save a quantity of information that would have been previously unimaginable. All that's required is that it be systematized so that the task of filing material in a useful way doesn't become onerous. The heaps of digital photos most of us have sitting on our hard drives are evidence that people aren't going to take to life-logging if it means we need to work really hard at organizing things. This is something the major tech companies understand. Services such as Apple's iCloud, for instance, mean that volumes of data can be stored in the cloud and accessed on any of your devices, relieving you of the burden of even thinking about syncing your information. In the fall of 2011, when Facebook announced its redesign around the idea of Facebook Timeline, they were acknowledging that they could now be, essentially, the repositories for people's digital lives. "Timeline is the story of your life," as Facebook honcho Mark Zuckerberg put it succinctly in announcing the new feature.

In some ways, a less extreme version of life-logging is already here. It's now normal for us to have digital records of all kinds of things we used to remember, so that we can access them on demand. No one thinks it's weird any more that we don't know the phone numbers of even our loved ones, for instance. Any event of even minor significance is photographed with a cellphone camera, and there are more and more tools for capturing daily information all the time. We are starting to take for granted that information about our lives is recorded and searchable. In 2002, writer Cory Doctorow characterized his blog as an "outboard brain,"[6] essentially, an ongoing scratchpad for anything he might need to access later. Increasingly, our digital devices can accompany us wherever we go. Aren't all of these assembled tools really just part of our outboard brain, more searchable than our own foggy memories would ever be?

Bell and Gemmell paint an appealing picture of how this searchable life might look and what it would allow us to accomplish. It's the kind of thing that ought to make any self-tracker's heart beat a little bit faster. "Click a button," they write, "and see a chart of how much exercise you have been doing in the last month, or year. Compare it to what you did when you were sixteen, or in the summer versus the winter."[7] Indeed, the physical fitness and health benefits to an übertracked life are clear. If I find it useful to get a weekly report from the RescueTime Robot breaking down how I am spending my time on the computer, why not break down how I'm spending my life? Welcome to, in Bell and Gemmell's words, the "e-memory revolution."

## THE DATA-MAPPED SELF:
## A CONTINUAL FEEDBACK LOOP

If people like Gordon Bell are right about a future of life-logging and constant capture, the real value is not just in the searchable database that my life has become, it's in the creation of a feedback loop between how I behave in the flesh-and-blood world and what my data-mapped self tells me. Right now, if I wear a pedometer and track my steps, then look at the graph of my progress over weeks and months, the whole point of the exercise is to alter my behaviour – in the belief that the act of monitoring and the feedback it generates are going to translate into actual behaviour change. I will walk more, which in turn means my data-generated, digital Nora also walks more, and the loop, the interchange of data and behaviours, continues. At this point, with the exception of life-logging outliers, most of us are choosing to apply these self-tracking techniques to specific areas of our lives. The power of the feedback loop between the digital self and the flesh-and-blood self could be useful indeed, once you can track just about everything. You can imagine a scenario in which we engineer feedback into our lives automatically. If our daily activity levels drop below a certain point, perhaps our daily available calories drop too – never find yourself with that sneaky extra bit of weight that you weren't expecting. If blood-sugar levels change, available menus could be altered to bring you back to a carefully calibrated level. Tracking and managing your health will be all the easier.

## QUESTIONING THE FUTURE

Jamais Cascio, a guy who may just have the best name ever, has coined a term for this world of constant self-observation: the Participatory Panopticon.[8] Cascio is a writer and thinker about emergent technologies who has looked at where these technologies may be taking us down the road. The Panopticon, you'll recall, was the prison surveillance system envisioned by Jeremy Bentham. Cascio argued with remarkable prescience (as far back as 2005) that we are moving into a time when we will all be tracking our own information like the life-loggers. His vision suggests we would use this monitoring to witness and share not just what we are doing but what *others* are doing, from monitoring police at demonstrations to calling up the exact words our spouse used on a particular occasion. Cascio projected ahead from the then-new world of cellphones-with-pretty-good-cameras to a future of PMAs, or Personal Memory Assistants, and saw a potential Pandora's box of concerns that would need to be addressed. It's worth looking at them, to illustrate the breadth of change we're talking about.

What happens when you go to the movies, for instance, an event we'll want to capture because we capture everything we do? "We'll undoubtedly see, initially at least, regulations demanding that people shut off their memory assistants while in movie theatres and such, or that the devices respect digital rights management and stop recording when copyrighted material comes on. But you know, if these devices become as widespread, as popular, and as useful as I expect them to be, you're going to eventually start getting pushback," Cascio told his audience at the MeshForum Conference in Chicago in 2005. The pushback may happen because people will be less willing to part with their experiences. The alternative, Cascio argues, is that we might end up with an unwieldy and intrusive extension of digital rights management such as "memory rights management," "where you have to have a license to remember."[8]

It sounds like science fiction, but it's actually just the far edge of a whole nest of questions associated with the coming data boom. It's perfectly reasonable for me to think that I "own" my experience, but our experiences are something that often we have as part of a collective. Do I have the right to keep and use your half of our conversation just because I have a small camera installed on the side of my glasses? In Cascio's particularly stark example, it's not unreasonable to assert that I own the experience of going to the movies, nor is it unreasonable to assert that my right stops when it means that I can replay essentially a pirated copy of that movie whenever I like. As Cascio points out, this is an issue we never had to consider when human memory's weakness meant all you were remembering was a snippet of a song. We might, though, imagine these kinds of conflicts coming up all the time over shared experience.

On the up side, Cascio argues, the presence of all that recording equipment offers the potential for a much more transparent society. He argues that personal recording at Abu Ghraib was a watershed "Rodney King" moment (and let's not forget that the images of Abu Ghraib were taken by the soldiers themselves, engaged in their own bizarre form of self-tracking). In Canada, we've seen the way video recordings of police actions at the G20 summit in Toronto in 2010 have led to a dramatic increase in transparency, whether police forces want it or not.

## THEY SEE YOU WHEN YOU'RE SLEEPING;
## THEY KNOW WHEN YOU'RE AWAKE

As I've suggested, digital technology has a particular character, which is that it "knows" how it's being used. That means we're essentially *enabling the technology to track us, simply by virtue of using it.* So far, we've mostly been concerned with our own efforts to track where we are and what we do, initiated by us, whether that's Gordon Bell using his MyLifeBits system or your pal tracking her jogging routine. But the reality is, using much digital technology, in effect, creates the opportunity for surveillance. This is the dual meaning of "self-tracking." How that information is stored, and who has access to it, has powerful, and even potentially dangerous, implications.

In the spring of 2011, Apple iPhone users were shocked to learn that information about their phone's location was being stored in the phone itself. The problem was that anyone who had physical possession of your phone, and the free, downloadable software to analyze it, could figure out with some accuracy where those phones – and hence the phone's users – had been. The justification, from Apple, at least, was pretty straightforward. In order to make the phone's service more efficient, it was keeping a record of Wi-Fi hotspots and cell towers near the phone's owner, and in any case, customers only needed to turn their Location Services function off to prevent the collection of this data. In the end, it seemed like an oversight more than anything else; location information was being transmitted to Apple every twelve hours anyway, so there was no reason to keep the data on the phone.[9] I think what registered with most users, though, was not an actual fear of someone finding out where you were; it was that uncanny feeling that just by using your phone, unbeknownst to you, there was a record of, more or less, where you had been. Expect these little privacy skirmishes to become a regular occurrence in the future, as we start to realize how much information our digital devices have about us. Right now, designers and companies choose what information to keep, where to keep it, and for how long, but as we go forward into a world of passively generated data, we will need to have a public discussion about these issues. We've decided, for instance, that you can't sell a car that doesn't have safety belts or a speedometer, because we have consensus that it would be unsafe to do so. The implications of storing location information on a phone run from law enforcement forensics, to the danger of stalking, to evidence in divorce proceedings.

Beyond the question of where the data is stored is the issue of who has access to it. For Nicholas Felton, the information designer and self-tracker, it's frustrating that the data being collected by his devices is out there but that he doesn't have access to it:

As someone who has tracked reading, it's something that's quite time-consuming and a little bit frustrating to do . . . I've started reading on my iPhone. And yet that data's not available to me in a time when it seems like everything else that can be done electronically has some data footprint or record that is available to me . . . like how many pages did I read or how long did I read yesterday . . . we're generating all these personal data streams [and] whether they're available to us or not, our data footprint is growing bigger and bigger.

Gordon Bell is way ahead of the rest of us, because he is helping to create the research tools that store information for him. By definition, he has access to all the information he's generating. For those of us who use off-the-shelf tools, we are going to have to consider how we are going to collate all that information. If I want those data sets to be searchable, they need to be available, but if various parts of my life-tracking are stored in incompatible formats spread across many different commercial systems, my Data Map is of more limited utility.

As regular users of these services, we tend to take for granted that they will always be there. But like any private company, they can go out of business or simply change business direction, leaving your data vulnerable. Whole chunks of your logged life – all those photos you put on Flickr, the record of the places you checked into on Foursquare – could disappear one day, if you're not quick enough on the draw to protect them. We need to ensure that we can get at our data, easily, whenever we want.

### ICANSTALKU.COM

At the 2010 HOPE hackers' conference, presenter Ben Jackson revealed something chilling. He showed that because smartphone photos are often geotagged, lots of people routinely post photos of themselves to their public Twitter profile that show people where they are. The researchers created a website called icanstalku.com, a feed of where various Twitterers are, posted to a Google Map. This revelation prompted a flurry of news stories pointing out that those fun pictures you posted to Facebook of your kid at the playground were location stamped. (It's a pretty simple matter to turn this function off, but you have to be aware that it's there in the first place.) Unlike Gordon Bell, for whom life-logging is a private activity, sharing information is part of what motivates many of us to create Data Maps of ourselves in the first place. We post the photos of our trip to the restaurant as a matter of course. We don't think about the fact that if we can put together our "data selves," so can other people. If most people seem to have trouble figuring out their Facebook privacy settings, how much more inadvertent oversharing is there likely to be as our digital trails grow? The very ease and automatic nature of so many of these tools means that we don't actually really have to understand how they work to use them. But if we don't understand how they work, we might not be using them prudently.

### A SEARCHABLE LIFE

One of the most intriguing questions for me in this vision of a life-logged future is a philosophical one: what does having a "searchable" life mean for memory? When our "outboard brains" are not storing only best friends' phone numbers, or countless images we've taken with our cellphone cameras, but pretty much everything, what does that mean for the act of remembering? Attending to information – remembering to remember it – is surely part of what makes memories meaningful to us. Some of the strongest memories I have, ones that have really shaped how I choose to live my life, are ones that weren't recorded. They're moments I remember as peak experiences, where I consciously told myself that an experience was fleeting and important and that I wanted to be able to bring it to mind. I remember a hot, dry walk in Sardinia years ago, for instance – the smell of the dry vegetation and the sound of the bells that the goats wore and the look of bougainvilleas. A searchable personal archive wouldn't be able to do anything like capturing the emotional quality of an event. Beyond that, will we even attend to remembering so much, if we know information is always accessible, or will we simply let it be captured, knowing that, like our friends' telephone numbers, memories will always be ready to hand?

In his excellent book *Delete: The Virtue of Forgetting in the Digital Age*, Viktor Mayer-Schönberger observes that human memory isn't like computer memory. "Recall is retrieving from a corpus of memories that is ever changing, and which is reconstructed by our mind to take into account subsequent experiences, preferences, and biases."[10] In short, he means that human memory is not only subjective, it is also informed by how life was lived afterwards. I worry that we will come to devalue this shape-shifter memory of ours as digital memory takes precedence. After all, which of those memories is really true: the objective facts, the literal words that were spoken during that long-ago breakup, or the more subjective narrative that evolves as my life changes, and I see things differently?

A colleague of mine, who is the parent of a young child, reflected on the fact that parents take so many digital photos that there is hardly a moment of a child's life today that is not documented. When we oldsters look at those few and far between pictures of ourselves – the faded image from an old birthday party, the holiday dinner where we sulked while everyone else said "cheese" – we read so much into it. It's like a portal to a highly subjective experience of our personal story. What will it mean for the generation who are just now very young, growing up in a world where that voluminous photo library is just one example of the documented life, accounted for and searchable? Perhaps they'll understand themselves better, more accurately, than we do now. But I wonder if they'll miss the reflection that comes from reminiscence, unchecked by the relentless rigour of the facts.

## STATUS (UPDATE) ANXIETY

In his satirical novel *Super Sad True Love Story*, author Gary Shteyngart paints a hilarious and frightening picture of what this world of constantly captured information could look like, assuming we bring our love of sharing along for the ride. In the world of the novel, people carry something called appäräts on their bodies at all times, which project their own personal details and allow them to see others': a mix of banal biographical facts, such as where a person went to school, with the hyperpersonal, such as sexual tastes and financial ranking. Shteyngart uses it to paint a picture of a society that distracts itself from confronting the existential fact of human mortality even as it uses technology to try to halt decline and death. It is a culture that treats the body as a hygiene project. In Shteyngart's insightful fictional world, people gaze joylessly at their appäräts, shopping compulsively, monitoring others' stats, and their own, because they cannot face death or, ultimately, life. They are constantly pushing themselves into the world around them, spitting out a tickertape of opinions, statistics, and minutiae, both banal and intimate. The vision Shteyngart portrays really is of people walking around with their Data Maps displayed, much as people online now have an avatar that represents them. In the real world, the boundary between what we share online and what we keep private seems to be moving in one direction only, toward being more public about our Data Maps. Perhaps you will start to look as if you have something to hide if you don't want to be public about your personal Data Map, in the same way that people are now routinely encouraged to have well-curated online identities, even if that shiny, impersonal simulacrum of a self doesn't really reflect the real you.

As a complete Data Map of the self starts to look more likely all the time, we'll need to deal with a lot of practical issues, but ultimately the biggest challenge may be in what it does to our self-understanding. On the one hand, a Data Map of what we did, how we felt, and what our bodies were doing presents us with a more "accurate" reading, less subject to the haze of memory or the way we would like to see ourselves. On the other hand, it takes us ever further into the realm of the objectified self. Not only are we written out and documented, we become a self that is comprised of statistical information. The risk is that this mapping takes us further away from a path of introspection, so that we are instead turning ourselves into projects that we tinker away on. The data-mapped life is a way of giving ourselves a certain coherence, a kind of constancy, but it's not the coherence you can get from a life lived in community, building a collective sense of meaning. Nor is it the sort of coherence you get from asking questions about your emotional and spiritual life. How could it, for those are precisely the things that the digital cannot measure.

We are becoming Marshall McLuhan's extended self, our brains, our nervous systems extended outside the body into digital space, existing in a real, flesh-and-blood world, but also in a parallel, digital world. There, we will be represented in the best way the computer knows: as numbers, as datasets, which can then be refined, visualized, and further objectified, as a splendid, pretty map.

[ SIX ]

# GOING SOCIAL
Your Data Map and the Coming Age of Big Data

Until now, we've been looking primarily at the individual: how much data each of us is starting to generate about our ordinary, everyday comings and goings. We talked about the factors – technological, psychological, and cultural – that have come together for this new era of self-tracking to take off. Because that information is digital, it can be rearranged. But it can also be aggregated, and that makes all the difference.

Since you and I are, collectively, creating information about the world around us – how we interact with it, what our reactions to it are –that information can be used for the social good. If the micro context is individual self-tracking, then the macro context is the aggregate of our information about how society is behaving. We're creating a collective Data Map, a constantly evolving, near real-time digital version of the world around us, based on all that information we're pushing out about ourselves. Just as we have our own digital doubles in our personal Data Map, we collectively have an aggregated, social Data Map. Like the personal Data Map, it is shareable, rearrangeable, and location-based. Just as we individually can gain personal insight by letting our digital tools track how we are using them, we may on a collective level gain social insight by accessing that information. I hope this collective Data Map will help us build smart, responsive communities. I hope it will change the way businesses operate, the way we plan cities, help us to understand the spread of disease and do research. Access to our data can change not only our individual lives but also our communities, and even our world. This is powerful stuff, but it won't be harnessed for social good without deft stick-handling and tough decisions along the way.

The buzzword *big data* refers to the growing existence of incredibly large data sets and the ability to analyze and make use of them. Big data might refer to the data that cellphone companies have about the habits of their customers, or all the data that Facebook has about the tastes and preferences and friendship groups of its hundreds of millions of users around the world. According to *Forbes* magazine's blog,[1] Walmart processes more than a million transactions per hour. That's a lot of customer data. Big data, though, also refers to the ability to manage that data and make it useful. All that data we're generating isn't worth much if it can't be analyzed *meaningfully*. Increasingly, we not only have access to lots of data, we have the processing power to store and make sense of it, so that although data mining has been around for a long time, its moment may finally have come. As businesses, researchers, and governments wrestle with what's been called "the data deluge,"[2] the push is on to harness the power of data. While these big data sets will come from many sources, from the point of view of the Data Map, what's fascinating is how much of that useful data, the sheer raw numbers, may come from citizens themselves. The aggregation of our data into useful, macro-level information comes down to three aspects of our self-tracking: what we contribute to collective maps by registering what we observe; what can be harvested from our self-tracking; and what is harvested using the passive data we generate by using our digital devices.

### AGGREGATING WHAT YOU SEE: THE POWER OF MAP-MAKING 2.0

In March 2010, journalist Marshall Kirkpatrick, in the *New York Times*,[3] described a cool little event, providing an elegantly simple example of the power of auto-reportage. Early one evening, citizens in Portland, Oregon, were treated to a sudden window-rattling boom. There was no immediate explanation for this unusual event. Folks began, as they do these days, tweeting about the sound and wondering what it was, using the hash tag #pdxboom (pdx being the code for the Portland airport, and airport codes being a common shorthand for identifying a location on Twitter). This is a common enough experience of auto-reporting on Twitter. When something unusual happens in my city, such as a power outage, the first thing I might do is tweet what is happening in my location. Invariably, others will respond, and we quickly get an idea of how widespread the problem is around the city. It's hardly a rock-solid survey and not a substitute for an official top-down explanation; it is, rather, a rough-and-ready tool for sharing your experience and seeing how others are affected almost immediately. In the Portland case, what the tweets turned up was that people in many locations throughout that city heard the sound, but the boom was louder or softer depending on where people were.

A local designer named Reid Beels had an idea. He created a Google Map to document that information. The map instructed interested citizens how to pinpoint on the map where they were when the boom hit and what it sounded like. In creating a map that everyone had access to and could add information to (by virtue of it being online and in a handy Web 2.0 form) Beels was able to take the individual, loose auto-reportage that happened on Twitter and make it much more precise, bringing it all together on a (literal) map. The next step was to make the map available to the people who could make effective use of the information. By getting descriptions of where the boom was the loudest, police narrowed their search. After investigating a local park, they were able to identify the source of the boom: a detonated pipe bomb.

The inchoate information that forms the bulk of what you see on Twitter – the more or less banal things people are inclined to tweet about (which skeptics typically deride as "telling everyone what you had for lunch") – is of marginal interest if you know the Tweeter personally, but otherwise is made up of a disorderly collage of individual real-time moments. In the right context, however, that personal reportage can be a powerful tool. Collectively, tweets, particularly when identified by topic through use of a hash tag, can seem like a kind of bottom-up, emergent intelligence, as users agree on a term and share information. How much more effective that emergent, collaborative picture can be, though, with the aid of an organizational tool, and some sort of analysis to make the most of this information. In this case, the key to turning the Portland tweets into effective information lay in one person's penny-drop recognition that the relative sound of the boom would be a good guide to location. Participants didn't need to know anything about where they thought the sound was, they didn't need to know what the sound was, only what the sound they heard was like, and where they were when they heard it.

This neat little news story shows us how the kind of auto-reporting we do as part of our self-tracking can work on a bigger, macro scale, and what some of its characteristics are. First, the information, by itself, was trivial. I heard a big boom – big deal! Second, it was easy to share with other people, first through the informal network of Twitter, then in a more structured way, on a map with a clear set of instructions. Third, it's the kind of information that would be difficult or time-consuming to gather by traditional, centralized means. Even if the Portland police had the money to investigate the source of the sound, going door to door asking people what they heard would have been very time-consuming. Fourth, the more people who participated, the better the quality of the information. If two people on a block participated, you'd have to be pretty confident in the accuracy of their observations. You'd have to know, for instance, that neither of them had unusually acute, or unusually poor, hearing. Finally, and crucially, it was easy to connect the information to a physical location: where a participant was when he or she heard the sound.

The Portland case is a good example of what the future could look like, where the information you relate about your own experience of the world around you can be coordinated and used for the social good. Your virtual representation of what is going on in real, physical space – that Data Map of the self we've been building – can be pooled with all those other Data Maps around specific types of information. We may not want to know the collective activities and observations of everyone in Portland at all times, but there are specific types of information (what that boom sounded like, and where) that can come in handy. Further, that shared information then has the potential to create a real-time feedback loop, which connects back to you in your window-rattled room at home. Imagine the explosion had not just been a single, detonated pipe bomb, but a crisis unfolding over time, such as a series of explosions. Wouldn't you want not just to contribute your voice and send it out via a random tweet, but to have access to the collective intelligence tracked on that map?

## THE DATA MAP:

## WHEN THE CARTOGRAPHER IS YOU

Simple auto-reportage can be aggregated and harnessed to useful, even inspiring, ends. The ability to create bottom-up maps is taking off all over the place, in simple but powerful tools. Sometimes, people contribute to those maps for altruistic or political reasons, and there's huge potential to develop this power as we carry more and more apps with us on our phones or have sensors of one kind or another dispersed in the environment. These don't need to be top-down government or corporate-funded endeavours. Pachube is an online platform designed to allow people to gather and display real-time information, in particular information that comes from sensors that are already in the world around us, such as pollution monitors or smart energy meters. After the earthquake and tsunami in Japan in March 2011, for instance, some engaged and tech-savvy citizens used Pachube to produce a real-time radiation map, based on the readings of individuals' Geiger counters. The existence of ready-to-hand tools such as Pachube means we have a new ability to create new maps and platforms quickly, to respond to a crisis or temporary situation. As exciting as this citizen engagement is, the more common use may lie in harnessing the enlightened self-interest of individuals, where generating information is useful to you personally, but also beneficial in the aggregate. Clever design will mean we needn't necessarily rely on citizens' active engagement or altruism.

A cool example of the relationship between personal self-tracking and the greater social good is Asthmapolis.

The GPS-enabled asthma inhaler tracks when and where a user takes a puff. That information allows the user personally to track his asthma conditions (correlating asthma triggers with inhaler use), and to see the information on a mobile map on his cellphone.[4] It's a classic example of how personal self-tracking can improve quality of life. At the same time, though, that data in the aggregate, linked as it is to real geographical locations, can help map asthma-related air-quality issues in the US Midwest, where it's being tried out. Here is the Data Map in action. As individuals carry out their self-interested self-tracking, they are generating useful information. The challenge lies in creating useful applications such as Asthmapolis; what are the sorts of individual activities that, when aggregated, might give us larger insights that would otherwise be too onerous or expensive to gather?

In some ways, dynamic maps aren't new. Researchers and governments have long kept tabs on citizens. Census data was collected in China as far back as 3000 BCE. Moreover, plotting people's movements and behaviours on maps for insights isn't new either. In his book *The Ghost Map*, science and technology writer Steven Johnson documents the London cholera outbreak of 1854. It was by mapping the movements of people amidst the outbreak that the connection was made between the spread of the disease and the use of a pump with contaminated water. Much as in our Portland example, the cholera detective work benefitted from what Johnson calls "local knowledge," embodied in the figure of Henry Whitehead, a clergyman who went around and assembled the data about people's movements. With the arrival of digital technology, we can now upload information ourselves, rather than rely on someone else to gather it for us, and, as in the Asthmapolis example, information gathered in one context, for one purpose, can be used in another – a feature that, as we'll see, is both beneficial and dangerous.

In the conclusion of *The Ghost Map*, Johnson touches on the power of connecting people's observations, movements, and behaviours to physical locations, citing examples like the 311 service in cities or people tagging Web-based information with location.[5] Unlike in Whitehead's era, it can be done quickly and on the fly from a cellphone, and plotted on the Web rather than a physical map. Johnson went on to help launch Outside.in, a website originally designed to aggregate information people were posting not about cities but about neighbourhoods – the kind of hyperlocal information that wouldn't make it into your daily newspaper. It required the creators of that information (who might be you or me, posting our photos to Flickr or writing about the construction down the street on our blogs) to tag the information they were creating with data about its location. The idea was to begin to yoke all the online information out there to real, physical locations, unleashing its power.

Outside.in may have been ahead of its time when it launched back in the olden days of 2006, but since then much has changed. The app revolution and the rapid spread of devices such as GPS-enabled cellphone cameras means that many people have the ability to post information that's tied to a physical location, sometimes without even being aware they are doing it.

The biggest impact of this collective Data Map right now is how it's playing out in business. As the auto-reportage of consumer experience takes off, businesses need to be much more responsive to customers, because information about those businesses is everywhere, continuously updated, and available at a moment's notice. Using customer review sites such as Urbanspoon, anyone can now look up reviews about the businesses that surround them as they stand on a street corner with a cellphone, and this keeps businesses on their toes. Businesses are even using *other* businesses' data sets to improve customer relations, and location-based data can help them do this more effectively. In the United States, AT&T began tracking Twitter reports of customers complaining about dropped calls and other such cellphone irritants, and then cross-referenced those reports with time and location information, in order to improve its performance.[6]

We're still in the early stages of making this sort of auto-reportage truly helpful. Greater participation will make results more accurate, rather than the opinion of a minority with an axe to grind. To make this sort of service really useful, though, we're going to need to design tools that are more finely grained. To find, say, a good Indian restaurant, I want access not just to the opinions of people who have reviewed nearby Indian restaurants but to those who have been to India and who also like other restaurants I enjoy. Search engines will get more sophisticated, tailoring results to who we are and where we are, and reporting on tastes, preferences, and "likes" will become more useful, but we are not there yet.

We're becoming a culture that is used to having our opinions and thoughts registered, whether that's for civic-minded purposes or to get back at a waiter for ignoring us. What we are creating is a map of our communities that is increasingly annotated with bottom-up, user-generated data, based on the almost incidental information individuals add about themselves. As we become urban cartographers, however, we are also turning ourselves into tightly defined target markets. We use tools and platforms run by businesses, and in registering our opinions, we define the products that will be marketed to us.

## THE BUSINESS OF INFORMATION: WHEN BIG DATA IS A BUSINESS PLAN

Once upon a time you needed to be some type of authority to create a big-picture look at how individuals' choices and behaviours translated into a social snapshot of the way we're living: a government gathering census information, say, or a university lab conducting a research study. Increasingly, though, all you seem to need is a start-up and a sufficient number of people to participate, because it turns out we're more than willing to share enough information about our behaviours to be statistically interesting. As long as a start-up offers a platform that is useful and engaging, we users will create the data. The services that sites are offering may differ but the end result is the same: we create data, and that data creates value.

Consider the example of Mint.com, the immensely popular personal finance website I mentioned earlier. Mint's business model lies in marketing financial services and deals to its subscribers. The site lists offers from financial institutions, customized to your particular financial situation, and collects a fee from those institutions when a Mint.com user switches to them. It makes recommendations based on information it has about various financial offers but maintains that the relationships it has with banks and financial institutions don't affect what offers you see.

It is no surprise that Mint.com has a lot of information about how its users spend their money. Late in 2010, Mint launched Mint Data, to release aggregate information about spending habits. Once a sufficient number of people were using Mint (according to Mint.com, users numbered over six million in the fall of 2011), it became possible to extract intriguing information from Mint's database, such as how much money people would spend on lunch in San Francisco versus lunch in Boise, Idaho, or useful tourist information, such as the most popular coffee shop in a particular locale, at least amongst those who use Mint. As I write this, Mint.com was giving away that aggregate information for free on its company blog, and it is unclear what, if anything, they plan to do with it, but it's intriguing to think of what could be done with this aggregate data.

For instance, the data in the aggregate may be useful and marketable to Mint users themselves (the budget-conscious person drinking expensive caffe lattes may be a prime market for, say, a cheaper coffee chain that boasts good-quality coffee). Understanding the spending habits of consumers in different markets could be very useful to national chains deciding how to market in various locales. The power of these analytics naturally depends in part on numbers. If their stats are skewed because they are pulled from a pool of people who are heavily engaged in monitoring their budgets, and tech-y enough to be comfortable monitoring those budgets online, then those stats are useful for advertisers who are targeting that group, but they can't be assumed to be representative of the broader public. If self-tracking becomes truly commonplace, however, as I believe it will, the numbers may be more generally useful.

Businesses that provide these online platforms can not only crunch the data consciously offered up by users, they can also do analytics based on the behaviour of users as they interact with the site, thanks to, you guessed it, the fact that digital technology knows how it's being used. Take, for example, the dating website OKCupid.com, which was started by four Harvard math grads. The site began releasing handy dating tips, which were based on the information people chose to put on their profiles combined with data on how other users of the service responded to those profiles, that is, data on the respondents' activity on the site rather than from the content of the information they entered. For instance, OKCupid.com released information about the kinds of profile photos that were most effective by, on the one hand, categorizing the types of photos, and, on the other hand, by seeing how many messages visitors to those profiles left. As an example, it turns out, in a shocking twist, that shots of women showing cleavage are actually popular!

Information can be brought together, then, even if users are not consciously trying to share information (beyond messaging another person on the site). Trust and terms-of-service agreements become important concepts here. The trend so far is going in only one direction: we are contributing more data, and that data is being displayed. The line between the data we are actively choosing to make available (our opinions, etc.) and the data we are generating passively (through our behaviour) is blurring.

## DATA EXHAUST AND DYNAMIC DEMOGRAPHICS

The term *data exhaust* refers to the byproducts of our online behaviour and interaction with digital devices, as opposed to the information we specifically choose to leave behind as we go about self-tracking. We saw how data exhaust might be useful in your personal Data Map, such as with my RescueTime productivity reports, but their aggregated, *social* use as part of our collective Data Map may be even more helpful.

The most obvious example of this is in the refinement of online search. Google provides you with search results more quickly, by sorting results based on what other people commonly search for. I'm not trying to help Google or my fellow computer users when I search, but all the same the byproduct of my searching is an improvement in the speed of search results for all. In addition, because one is searching from a computer, and a computer has an IP address, Google can tell where searches are likely coming from. Once the volume of searches is large enough to be statistically significant, it can be very revealing of what's going on in the real, physical world. By locating where people are searching for flu information, for instance, Google has created Flu Trends, which reveals how flu-like symptoms are migrating. Evidence suggests that while Flu Trends is accurate at predicting flu-like symptoms (which may be due to illness other than flu, such as colds), it's not as accurate in predicting where influenza will turn up as actual flu data. These results are hardly surprising, but they do suggest that data exhaust needs to be used with care.

Right now, aggregated information – about finances, or dating profiles, or search behaviours – is for the most part a sort of data-based curio. It's a patchwork of data sets and analytics. But what if you could bring these data sets together in a more systematic way? Think of flu trends or purchasing behaviour or Geiger counter readings as micro-level examples of what we might envision and you can see how this information might come together to create a truly complete Data Map: a highly dynamic, responsive picture of both the data that we produce intentionally, and what we produce inadvertently. How much of our decision-making as individuals, never mind as urban planners, or as national leaders, is held back by a lack of access to information, by a lack of knowledge of how a system was being used? Can we instead harness that data to build smarter cities?

## COGNITIVE CITIES

What would it mean if, just as our digital tools now know how they are being used, *the city itself* knew how it was being used? You can think of the city as a technology, actually. It's a set of systems – transportation, power, water, parks, garbage collection, libraries, food importing and sales – which allow people to live, play, and work together in a contained geographic space. We have a periodic census that shows us things like income distribution and number of people in a home with a computer. We do occasional updates to show how the roadways are being used, by counting the number of vehicles going over it for a period of time, but that information is still mostly static. The advantage of the kind of continually updated information that the Data Map describes is that it gives us what researcher Alex (Sandy) Pentland has described as "dynamic demographics,"[7] data based on how people are *actually* moving, rather than how we assume they are.

We are now seeing a lot of research into how a continually updated, collective Data Map might work. This kind of Data Map goes under various names – Smart Cities, Cognitive Cities, Urban Computing, IBM's "smarter planet" – all centred around the idea that a city that is alive with continually updated information can be more sustainable and efficient and can better serve the needs of its residents.

I decided to visit MIT's SENSEable City Laboratory, which is at the forefront of research into the future of cognitive cities. I arrived in Cambridge on a beautiful, autumn day. For any technology journalist, the Massachusetts Institute of Technology is kind of the Holy Land, and it was a particular thrill to walk across the Charles River and head to the SENSEable City Lab. As someone with a liberal arts education, I have certain associations with the word "lab" that weren't borne out by the fairly modest setting, with researchers plonked down here and there, working away on laptops, and not a white lab coat to be seen. The lab is an interdisciplinary research group that explores how to harness data about how people use the city they live in, in order to make those cities more sustainable and also more responsive to how residents actually use the urban environment. This knowledge could benefit areas such as tourism, event management, and urban planning. As they describe the context of their work at the lab's website: "The way we describe and understand cities is being radically transformed – alongside the tools we use to design them and impact on their physical structure."[8] Studying and "anticipating" those changes is the goal of the lab.

I met with Francesco Calabrese, a computer scientist at the lab. He was leading a research project called Network & Society, whose aim is to employ large data sets to "explore physical mobility, social networks and urban places."[9] Of particular use in his research is cellphone data. Basically, by analyzing (anonymized) data about where people are going (which one can tell by the relationship of the phone to nearby cellphone towers) and the pattern of phone calls (as opposed to the content of those calls) it's possible to get a much better idea of what people's needs are in a city and then to respond to meet those needs. He tells me:

Through the technology . . . the whole city environment can be adjusted in a timely fashion . . . There will be improvement from the point of view of city management, . . . the city will know a lot more about the mobility system, event management, how tourism works . . . Money can be spent . . . on what works.

Information gathered this way could be helpful for building more sustainable cities, for instance. Calabrese talked to me about how you could use it to test the idea that having basic services distributed throughout neighbourhoods reduces the need to travel, again, based on information gathered from the patterns of mobile phone use. An obvious use of this kind of tracking is in improving traffic flows, or in assessing where to build large public buildings so they cause a minimum of traffic disruption.[10]

In his research, Calabrese uses the kinds of information generated simply by using a cellphone, but he also uses data, such as geotagged photos that tourists upload to the photo-sharing website Flickr. He argues that intentionally generated data is more meaningful, since with it "[people] share more of their lives." And he sees it as a trend that is only going to continue:

> You can feel that there are more and more people that use these smart phones, and more and more people that use them to share information with others; we see there is this growing trend.

Of course, it's desirable to have as broad a picture as possible, not simply one that comes from early adopters. As Calabrese pointed out to me, this may affect where you do research. Americans, for instance, seem to be more eager than Europeans to adopt web-based services such as Flickr.

The key to getting that broad picture is access: the SENSEable City Lab's vision relies making data available for research. This poses a challenge: much of the data is being gathered by private corporations, who may have an interest in keeping that data to themselves, thank you very much. As Calabrese told me:

Companies know a lot about their customers, especially for marketing purposes. Actually, at least as far as we know, they never thought about using the same information for service for the general public . . . for the common good. They're concerned about their profit . . . Working with them, we're showing them . . . that it's not just to increase their market share, . . . [it's] to provide service.

A truly smart city would draw on all kinds of information, then, not just the data generated by users. Self-tracking is only one factor in creating these cities of the future. Smart cities would use, for example, sensors to communicate updates about city services. We already have embryonic examples of how this works. My hometown of Toronto, for instance, has been experimenting with real-time updates along some streetcar and bus routes. Because the vehicles are equipped with GPS, they can communicate that information to an updatable sign at the stop, providing continually updated schedules. That's just one small example of how sensors can play a role in making a dynamic, responsive city possible.

Unquestionably, though, the tracking information we citizens generate is going to be key in the smart city, particularly information from our cellphones. It's the most obvious, elegant way to gather information about movement and location. Cellphones are also approaching near-ubiquity in many parts of the world, and increasingly, income is not an impediment to cellphone use. About 60 per cent of people in sub-Saharan Africa had access to cellphones in 2010, and worldwide cellphone subscriptions topped 5 billion that same year. Even basic model cellphones without GPS capability can be good trackers of human movement, because their location is correlated to the nearest cellphone tower.

Alex Pentland is another researcher at MIT (though not at the SENSEable City Lab) working in this area. He calls what he does "reality mining," and it relies specifically on the information available through cellphones. He has argued that the behavioral data that comes from tracking cellphones is particularly valuable in areas of the world where demographic data from sources such as a census can often be in short supply.[11] Pentland describes the power of the mobile phone in leaving "digital breadcrumbs" behind that can be analyzed.[12] Reality mining hopes to track not only movement but also things like the patterns of who users call and text, in order to build an understanding of social relationships. One of the more frequently cited uses of this kind of information is in health research. It should provide more accurate information about the spread of communicable diseases such as SARS or flu; Pentland suggests it can be used to understand health risks for particular subpopulations.[13]

This kind of research obviously raises red flags for many of us. Fears of compromised privacy and abuse of data are the most obvious concerns. The collection of this kind of information about behaviour can sound at best like nannyism, and at worst like an intrusive Big Brother dystopia. It does suggest, though, how far analysis of patterns of movement and behaviour might be able to take us, individually and collectively. As we'll explore later, the rules governing the use of data will need to be strictly regulated, to protect privacy. Anonymized data is still valuable. A subtler question is what information individuals will voluntarily choose to make available, whether that's for altruistic reasons or personal gain.

For much of our history, a lack of access to information has structured our social institutions. The lack of access to information has shaped the way we work, date, educate our children, and socialize. When information is no longer scarce, institutions change, and social norms change with them. Consider, at one simple level, the difference that having cellphones has made to the way people socialize. People used to make fixed plans to meet at a given time and place. Being late for such an appointment was a big faux pas, because it left the person you were meeting just sitting there, cooling her heels. Now that we can be in touch via cellphone whenever we want, many of us constantly rejig our plans. The etiquette and social mores around being late are changing, because access to information about where you are has changed the consequences of being late. If a simple cellphone call can change social relationships, imagine what the sort of wholesale access to information we're looking at might do.

## BIRDS OF A FEATHER

While there are obviously a lot of benefits to the smart city, one of the great pleasures of city life is the serendipitous, the random, the unexpected. A city that is constantly updated with information is a city that avoids frustration, but it's also a city that avoids happy accidents.

This is not merely a romantic observation. In a city that is entirely knowable, flooded with information, we will have access to tailored versions of what the city around us *means*. If it's already true that the reader of The Economist has a different idea about the meaning of an event than the reader of People magazine, how much more will that be the case in a data-soaked city? My city will be informed by the opinions, tastes, and preferences of those who think like I do. Harvard Internet researcher Ethan Zuckerman has described this as the problem of homophily online.[14] Already, we have this "birds of a feather" problem with the way we consume information on the Web. We may like to think of ourselves as voracious readers online, but we tend to read things that come from our part of the world, from our perspective. What will that be like when we carry our customized informational world around with us? We won't be looking at a shared map; we'll have individual maps, based on our interests, our friends, based on "birds of a feather."

When we visit a city with a conflicted history, let's say, Derry in Northern Ireland, what locations "mean," where you ought to go or ought to avoid, depends very much on who is showing you around. The whole experience of the city depends on the context you bring to it, and in a real way, in a city with a conflicted history, people inhabit *different* cities. I can't help but feel that as much as social software like Foursquare position themselves as "discovery" tools, what they are really doing is reinforcing bias. If I learn about my city based on where my pals on Foursquare go, I'm not going to learn about where people I don't follow go, people who may have a very different view of the city than my Foursquare friends.

The challenge, as we move toward a fully realized Data Map, at the personal level and at the societal level, lies in using it correctly. There is much at stake. Data Maps can teach us a lot about our own lives, and about how we behave as communities. But they also raise the chilling prospect of being slaves to our data. If we don't wrestle with the thorny issues around who owns the data, how to use it wisely, and how to protect privacy, the Data Map could be used to control us, to limit our freedom, and to subject us to a world of both surveillance and censoring self-surveillance. As I've said, the Data Map will contain many types of data, from many sources, but the data we generate will be a core part of that information ecosystem. It's time for us to think about the role we choose to play in the Data Map: how much of our information we want to contribute, and how actively we want our conscious self-tracking to become part of that map. I would love to see us as citizens participating actively, becoming cartographers in this new world rather than passive participants.

Bit by bit, the pieces of the Data Map are coming together, and we are largely ignoring the implications of it, blithely turning over our data to private corporations. Briefly we balk

when there is yet another privacy breach, yet another example of our data being used in risky or invasive ways, and yet
we always return, feeding our data back to the grid. It's time
for us to wake up to the dangers inherent in the Data Map,
because it's only in protecting ourselves from those dangers
that we can use the Data Map to its full potential.

# SEVEN

# LOOKING FOR A MEANINGFUL RELATIONSHIP
## Making Data Make Sense

A while back, I had a chance to chat with a public librarian about what we might do with all this data that we're generating. Public libraries, of course, have lots of information about their users, along with a rock-solid mandate to protect the information privacy of those same library users. She was skeptical about the power of the data boom: what is the use of all that data, if you can't figure out what it's telling you? It's a good point. What's the good of all that loyalty card–swiping, cellphone-calling, footstep-tracking behaviour, if it can't be transformed into useful information? That's why the push is on not just to crunch the numbers but to find ways to make the story that data tells comprehensible. Hal Varian, chief economist at Google, has suggested that the sexy tech job in the future will be statistician, of all things, someone who can take data and "be able to understand it, to process it, to extract value from it, to visualize it, to communicate it."[1] I would go one step further to suggest that the degree a young person really wants to get is a double major in statistics and visual arts. After all, we want our Data Map to be useful not just to experts but to you and me; data becomes most useful for non-expert citizens when it is simplified so that the story it tells is clear, without either being too reductionist or presuming too much. Visualizations will help us wrangle our own personal self-tracking and make sense of the collective tracking we're starting to do as a society.

I've been using the idea of a data "map" metaphorically, but creating compelling visual representations of data is an important step in making that information useful. Turning data into a comprehensible map, through data visualization, may not scream sex appeal. All the same, we'll need good visual tools to make data relevant. As powerful as I think the data is, it's all too easy to misinterpret it, whether inadvertently or under the sway of a political agenda. Data is seductive, because numbers are definite. Meaning, however, can be much more slippery. Because we are a society that loves numbers, we need to be clear about the conclusions and inferences we make from data and about when it actually leads us to jump to conclusions. We are about to put enormous faith in the power of the Data Map; we need to make sure it's telling us the truth.

We tend to think of maps as neutral tools, fact-based, scientific even. Maps though, are a reflection of the culture they are made in. They may be overtly political or ideological, for instance. Even with the best of intentions, no map shows absolutely everything, and the choices of what is worthy of depiction on a map speak volumes about a society. In Europe in the medieval period, for instance, maps were very different from our maps today. *Mappae mundi* weren't used to guide travellers to a location; they were educational tools, the flow charts of their age. They gave a kind of handy summary of important information about human history, and they reflected the way the medievals saw the world. Although they depicted geographical locations, that was not their primary function. The size of cities and land masses was determined not by strict geographic reality but by the significance of the territory in question. So, the Holy Land, for instance, was depicted both as much larger proportionately than it was in reality, and also in the centre of the map.[2] As Evelyn Edson describes the famous Hereford *mappa mundi* in her book *The World Map 1300–1492*, "the map was thus organized for the reader or student of sacred history who wished to imagine a pilgrimage or to arrange his meditations in spatial terms."[3] The whole understanding of how time ought to be depicted on a map was different, too. We think of maps as snapshots of what existed at a particular time but because the *mappae mundi* served a different function, they existed almost in an eternal *now*. Events at various historical times existed in the same spatial plane. Rather than north, the top of maps like the Hereford *mappa mundi*, Edson explains, pointed east, where you would find the Garden of Eden. On the same map you would find biblical events that were supposed to have happened later. Moving down the map toward the west, for instance, you would find Jerusalem and the image of the Crucifixion.[4] As befits people who were not yet run by the clock and the calendar, the way we moderns are, the very sense of how time and space ought to be placed on a visual aid was different.

As a digital culture, that which is best mapped is that which is best understood in digital terms, that which can be counted in discrete bits, that which can be enumerated. We, too, also live in an eternal now. Our data is continually updated; we don't even have to hit "refresh" any more. We speak of information as carried in feeds and streams and flows as though we are awash in it, carried along on a river of data. It is a reflection of the world as we understand it, every bit as much as the *mappae mundi* reflected the medieval worldview. The Data Map illuminates, but in choosing to highlight the digital, it also leaves parts of reality obscured. Here be dragons!

## THE CARTOGRAPHER'S APPRENTICE

It's surely a sign of pop culture's geek chic that one of the big trends these days is . . . graphs. Yes, whether it's graphs, grids, maps, charts, or Venn diagrams, the world of data visualization and infographics is exploding in popularity. Check out leading online news organizations and get a load of the gorgeous graphs and charts being used. The BBC and *The New York Times* are just two of the leading news organizations beefing up "data journalism,"[5] which is, essentially, telling stories through visualizations rather than narrative text. There are infographic rock stars, such as information designer David McCandless, who keeps the popular Information Is Beautiful blog and has written a book on the subject, or the team of Fernanda Viégas and Martin Wattenberg, who lead Google's "Big Picture" group on data visualization. Nicholas Felton, himself a star in the world of information design (he and his Daytum.com co-founder were hired by Facebook for their infographic acumen), told me that it seems like every graphics student is coming out with an infographic as part of his or her portfolio. Data visualization is so hot because of the push to make large data sets comprehensible to people who aren't experts, that is, you and me. That means translating statistics into simple, easy-to-digest visualizations, taking detailed information and generalizing it into a trend, for instance, but also making it possible to "drill down" deeper into the data to get more specific information. In his documentary *Journalism in the Age of Data*, Geoff McGhee documents smart journalistic uses of digital's power to reframe information to tell compelling stories, such as a *New York Times* graphic that compared US government deficit projections over a four-year period with the reality of the deficits over the same four years.[6] This is the kind of information a journalist could dig up and put into conventional narrative form, but it's much more striking and persuasive as a graphic that readers can look at and interact with. As we start to see the rise of smart cities where, ideally, citizens will have access to information about the community around them, we'll need infographics that are accurate and easy for citizens to understand.

Today's infographics differ in two ways from the ordinary old graphs you learned to make in school: regular people without special training now have the ability to make and share their infographics online, and those infographics are often dynamic and interactive. When infographics are online, they can do something graphs and charts on a page can't: move. Hans Rosling has become famous, in the niche-y Internet sense of famous, based not on what he technically does for a living – he's a professor of public health science in Sweden – but for his enlightening use of dynamic, interactive infographics. He's one of the founders of the Gapminder Foundation (tag line: "Gapminder: for a fact-based world view"), which is responsible for infographics software that displays statistical data as coloured circles plotted on an $x$-$y$ plane. Big deal, right? What makes it so striking, though, is that it's animated, so that you see data change, to remarkable effect. One of the most incredible examples of this animation in action is the one Rosling uses to show the life expectancy and fertility rate in various countries as they unfold over time. Watching the infographic, as Rosling presented it at a TED talk, dismantles our developed-world assumptions about a hard line between a prosperous "First World" and a permanently impoverished, benighted "Third World"; we watch countries' life expectancies rise and numbers of children decrease in the developing world (with the heartbreaking exception of parts of sub-Saharan Africa, where the AIDS epidemic meant life expectancy dropped suddenly, leaving it behind much of the rest of the world). Rosling wants to shatter those us-and-them developing/developed world clichés, and his infographic is the tool to do it. It's not that this information was not publicly available before – they're stats from the United Nations – it's that seeing it in a visual, accessible context means that it's suddenly meaningful, revelatory. It's even, I would say, *moving*. Not bad for a graph.

Rosling's use of visualization is a great example of what we need to do to make all this data work for us. It's one thing to have a lot of public data and quite another to have it in a form that is accessible, useful, and easy to understand. This is one of the driving forces in the "open data" movement, which pushes governments to make their statistical data and public service information available to the public. It's not about whether I can technically go to City Hall and pick up a pamphlet, or look at a list of information on a government website, but about whether it's in a useful format. Is it searchable? Can third parties design apps for it, for instance, so the data can be plotted on a Google Map? To take a simple example, in my own city of Toronto, a handy app for the iPhone allows cyclists access to a bicycle map and to display the information in multiple useful formats. This is not the kind of handy little tool that municipal governments need to spend taxpayer dollars to make. An entrepreneurial or civic-minded third party can make it, and in this case, did.

Welcome to the booming world of data visualization: the art and science of displaying information effectively and accurately. We humans are visual creatures. As data visualization designer Fernanda Viégas explained it to me on an episode of *Spark*, data visualization "allows you to very quickly get a sense of a lot of data . . . it gives you an overview of hundreds, lots of times thousands, of data points all at once, and because of the way our brains are built, we're very good at looking at patterns visually."[7] More importantly, in terms of preserving the meaningfulness of the data, visualization keeps the information within context. "One of the things that visualization does very well is paint a very broad picture and then allow you, from that broad picture, to zoom into details and data points, but the data points are always contextualized."[8] That is, you can get more and more finely grained with your data set, but the data is not removed from the context in which it was originally correlated.

Beyond making beautiful visualizations of existing data, designers are creating off-the-shelf services that make it easy for you and me to turn our data – large or small, personal or in the public interest – into visualizations of our own. Recall that part of the appeal of self-tracking lies in the fact that web-based services allow you not only to post your data, but to see it in visually stunning ways. In my own little corner of the data-visualization and self-tracking world on Daytum.com, where I tracked how often I brought my lunch to work instead of buying it, it's easy and kind of fun to focus on changing the pie chart that tracked the relative amounts of bought/brought, so that the "bought" slice of the pie got smaller and smaller. Our long historical fascination with maps, charts, and graphs suggests that we've always had an appetite for visualizations and found them helpful as a way to assimilate volumes of information, but Web 2.0 tools mean that everyone can get in on the game, regardless of what we choose to map. More importantly, those graphics can be publicly shared with others. IBM, for instance, runs a project called Many Eyes,[9] which Fernanda Viégas created, along with Martin Wattenberg. It allows anyone to load a data set and anonymously display it in one of many visualization types. It could be the sort of personal information we are collecting as self-trackers, of course, but many people use it to make persuasive, political visualizations, such as the one I saw depicting the amount of money donated to Pakistan by country, in the wake of flooding there. Thus it becomes a *social* tool, not just a personal one. As Viégas put it to me,

> people would really get into the analysis and the more powerful aspects of visualization when they were sharing these visualizations with others, and when they were actually having conversations around the kinds of things they were seeing . . .

As Viégas points out, sharing and interacting with data can be an important part of facilitating conversation about the meaning of information. Viégas is surely right that humans are visual creatures, and projects such as Many Eyes may help in the democratization of political debate. Certainly, we are sufficiently in love with the power of numbers as a culture that we're prone to be swayed by them. But therein lies a problem. Numbers don't always tell the whole story; they can be manipulated, or misunderstood. How much more effectively misleading can numbers be, in our data-drunk culture, when they're presented as eye candy?

## LIES, DAMNED LIES, AND STATISTICS

In the annals of jargon, "statistical literacy" – basically, the ability to read and understand the meaning of statistics – is admittedly an unlikely hot buzzword, and yet, as floods of data play an ever more important part in our lives, buzzword it is. In the fall of 2010, *Wired* magazine listed it as one of the "7 Essential Skills You Didn't Learn in College,"[10] and Andrew Alexander, writing in *The Washington Post*, has talked about the need for journalists, in particular, to understand statistics in our data-focused world.[11] We need to bring critical thinking skills to data, even, perhaps especially, when that data is visually appealing.

In practising statistical literacy, first of all, we need to ask about the value of the raw data itself. In the summer of 2010 in Canada, we had our own debate about the value of data, in "Censusgate." As the governing Conservative party moved to abolish the long-form Census, substituting it with a mandatory short census and a voluntary long-form census, we had an actual intense, public debate about the value of voluntary census data. In another era, data reliability might seem like a weird hot-button issue, but when data is used to make public policy, it has real political and social consequences. Part of the argument in Censusgate turned on the question of how public service providers and government departments could accurately organize resources if they didn't know the composition and needs of people for whom they were providing services.[12] How much more fraught will the reliability of data be, in an era of real-time data about the community around you? If we're making decisions about where to direct public resources based on data sets, it had better be accurate. The Great Canadian Census Debate points to a question about self-tracking more generally. At what point do the numbers of self-trackers, or the amount of data exhaust being generated, become statistically reliable? I have enough respect for statisticians, epidemiologists, and the like to be confident that public policy won't be affected by overvaluing the self-reporting of individuals, but what about more informal, less statistically literate uses of self-tracking data? My belief is that self-tracking and data exhaust from digital devices will at some point come to be so commonplace that they will represent what "people" are doing and thinking, rather than what early adopters are thinking and doing, but we need to remain critically minded about the accuracy of the data we're getting, even as we come to rely on it more and more.

## THE POLITICS OF MAPS

The accuracy of data sets is a technical issue, but we also need to wrestle with the thornier problem of the ideological misuse of data. The history of cartography is littered with stories of maps used for political ends. The very image of the map of the world has been criticized as political. In choosing how to display a 3D world on a 2D map, our commonly used map of the world ends up depicting Africa as much smaller than it is, and northern countries as much larger than they actually are. If, as I argue, map-making involves making judgements about what is worth depicting, we have to question what's left out of those beautiful visualizations.

When I asked Viégas about the politics of infographics in our *Spark* interview, she was upfront about what some of the dangers and challenges are:

> Any sort of representation is a framing of reality. Data visualization is visualizing numbers. People love to say, "Well, those are the facts." The truth is, that's a framing of reality too, because . . . there is a lot of, "We chose to measure this thing as opposed to that thing" . . . That's on the data side. On the presentation side, you can do all sorts of things to make certain things look better or worse . . . these are different ways of telling the same story. It's the same data and yet you end up with radically different images of the same story of the same data.

## DEDUCING, OR JUMPING TO CONCLUSIONS?

As Viégas points out, the decision to gather information about one area and not another can lead to a particular framing of reality, and the decision to display it one way or another can influence what it seems to mean. But even if no one is intending to mislead, can we always trust the story the data appears to tell us? Any scientist will tell you that you shouldn't confuse correlation with causation, but the very virtue of digital information – how easy it is to recontextualize – opens up a whole new can of worms, particularly when it's public. Nothing seems as unambiguously a good thing as making as much data available as publicly as possible, but maybe it's not as simple as that.

Lawrence Lessig is a law professor at Harvard with a

specialty in technology and law. He is active in issues of copyright reform for a digital age and sits on the advisory board of the Sunlight Foundation, a non-profit organization that tries to use the tools of the Internet to encourage greater government transparency. He's the kind of guy that many online activists – believers in copyright reform, Web 2.0, bottom-up culture, net neutrality – love, so it was a shock to some that in the fall of 2009, he wrote an influential and much-discussed article in *The New Republic* called "Against Transparency."[13] Transparency, in 2009, was a very hot topic. Barack Obama was still in his heady first year. Governments, in particular, ought to be transparent, went the mantra. Data should be open; voting records should be easily accessible. In the midst of this, Lessig argued that data transparency can be misleading, particularly "naked" transparency – pushing data out into the public, for journalists, citizens, whomever, to look at. He used the example of Hillary Clinton. When Clinton was still First Lady, she was publicly opposed to a bill called the Bankruptcy Abuse Prevention and Customer Protection Act. Once she became Senator Clinton, however, she voted for the same bill twice. (For the record, according to Lessig, she switched her vote again four years later.) She also happened to have received $140,000 in campaign contributions from the likes of credit card companies and other financial institutions. In a world where things like voting records and campaign contributions are made public, and correlated with other data sets, we can make inferences about what we think that data means, but are those inferences accurate? Does correlation equal causation? Lessig's point is that data can simply be deceiving, that perhaps there is in fact some other, more compelling explanation that is either not supported by data sets (maybe she had a credit card–related epiphany), or that there is some more relevant correlation of data that has not been included (the relationship between her voting record and her time as a New York senator, he suggests, as opposed to her opinions as First Lady). The problem is that data purports to be objective, but it comes with a very human backdrop of assumptions, and a "frame" or shorthand that we all go through life with. "At this time the judgment that Washington is all about money is so wide and so deep," Lessig wrote, "that among all the possible reasons to explain something puzzling, money is the first, and most likely the last, explanation that will be given."[14]

The problem of inference and the kind of shorthand that we tend to rely on, Lessig goes on to argue, is compounded by a simple practical problem: who, in this magical era of transparency, actually has the time to sift through the stacks of free data, performing the kind of sophisticated forensics necessary to draw accurate conclusions and rule out misapprehensions? Lessig's cautionary tale is the dark flip side to the power of digital to pump out so much information, and to correlate it easily with other data, in a way that would have been impossible in an analog era. There have always been investigative journalists who dig deep to connect the dots about politicians, but the same easy accessibility that we love about open data, Lessig's message shows us, can also allow for easy, sloppy assumptions.

The real danger that underlies the reliability of visualizations is not that we jump to conclusions, it's the way we take such comfort in their seeming certainty. They're numbers! It's objective! We don't consider the ideological framework that surrounds the collection and display of the information. Data is a powerful tool, but we have to remember that it's braided through with very human, very subjective assumptions.

## NETWORK ANALYSIS AND
## THE PROBLEM OF INFERENCE

Lessig's example points out the dangers of inferring too much from the data itself. When it comes to misinterpreting data, though, there's the content of the information itself but also the implicit information that is revealed by the way that the information flows. In fact, there's a whole field of study, social network analysis, built on analyzing just this sort of pattern of information flows amongst people. Social network analysis can reveal how groups work, where bottlenecks are, and the roles individuals play within groups. Researchers in this field don't care so much *what* you talked about on the phone, for instance; they care about the pattern of those calls. This is particularly true for analyzing human communication patterns, and so it becomes interesting in light of our culture of self-tracking. This kind of analysis doesn't require digital tools, but for all the reasons we've been discussing, it's easier to do when the information flows are registered digitally. I could spy on you and keep a record of whom you spoke to and where you were when you did so, but it would be a heck of a lot easier if I just had access to your cellphone records. You can make a lot of useful inferences about what the pattern of people's information flows indicates about them, but the important thing to remember is that they *are* inferences.

Let's look at a practical example of inference at work. *The Economist* magazine has written about the network analysis efforts of telcos in the United Kingdom to identify high-priority customers, so-called "influencers," the kind of well-connected people who are more likely to convince friends, colleagues, and family to change service providers when they themselves do.[15] They did this not by asking people how influential they thought they were, or by listening in on the content of their calls, but simply by observing the *pattern* of those calls. People with more clout or "social capital," it's argued, tend to do things like make long phone calls, but have short calls when someone calls them. They do not seem to be averse to making late-night calls. Turns out, influencers have a lot in common with the merely annoying. Once these influencers are identified, they can be targeted, says *The Economist*, with sweet deals – all the better to keep those important customers and hence to prevent them from changing the minds of the poor saps who aren't getting any such preferential treatment.

When we think about privacy, our first impulse is to think about content. We don't tend to think about information as a pattern, or the value of pattern recognition. The telcos weren't interested in intruding into the content of messages – what you said, or even to whom you said it. The fact that what they were looking at was "front of the envelope" information, such as whether you're ringing people up late at night or not, doesn't mean we shouldn't be concerned about the implications of this level of data analysis.

Of course, there might well be circumstances in which this profiling is warranted, such as, The Economist suggests, when narrowing down where a crime is likely to take place. Most of us probably assume that businesses gather metrics about their own customer base. They can also gather information about their employees' information flows, since they have the records: emails sent on corporate accounts, attachments sent, who has accessed the same information on the LAN, how phone calls flow. Analysis can go further, however, into analyzing behaviour patterns that, you guessed it, we are contributing voluntarily as part of our self-tracking behaviour. At the research level, this is what's being "reality mined" by Alex Pentland at MIT, by observing the movements and interactions of volunteers, based on their cellphone use.

While this information can be revealing, I learned how easy it can be to misinterpret or overstate what the data tells you, when I interviewed Valdis Krebs, for Spark. Valdis is a leading social network analyst. He himself creates visualizations of networks of communication. They look something like a map of airplane routes, with more activity around major airport hubs. It may be surprising for someone in his line of work, but Krebs sees real pitfalls in relying too quickly on what the data seems to show. In his work with organizations, Valdis uses an iterative process, essentially testing hypotheses about what is actually going on, to verify the explanatory power of his maps. He told me that he worries about what the sloppy use of social network analysis can do. Essentially, if you're not trained and careful about it, you can jump to conclusions:

I'm very concerned because I know what you can do with this data and I also know how you can misinterpret the data because I've seen people do that. I've seen people take data and jump to all sorts of conclusions that they have no right to, but they think, "Well, I have enough data to do that," and they're wrong . . . They have a view of how they see the world and they try to match the data to that view. And they often see patterns that may not be there or may not have that much meaning, but it supports how they see things . . .

What makes this a pressing concern is that inferences are being made about people based on information that's freely available on the Internet, including, of course, what we choose to report about ourselves as we go about our self-tracking behaviour. According to *The Economist*, "The raw data used may extend far beyond phone records to encompass information available from private and governmental entities, and internet sources such as Facebook."

I asked Valdis what he could tell about me based on the information I choose to put online:

What's easily available about you would be things like . . . your friends on Facebook, probably your colleagues on LinkedIn, the people you interact with on Twitter, so we could probably draw a fairly reasonable network neighbourhood around you. But there might be certain people around you that you're very close to that don't participate in these sites, and so we'll miss those. And unfortunately . . . people think, well, if they get your Facebook, they get your

LinkedIn, they get your Twitter and maybe your Foursquare information, they have a complete picture of you, and it's not true . . .

Even if you look beyond those (for now, at least) haphazard trails on online social networks, you can still misinterpret what the data means:

A *government*, they can start looking at your phone, they can start looking at your emails, they can start looking at all sorts of things. So they can get a more complete picture . . . If your network neighbourhood intersects with mine, well, that's fine. But if your network neighbourhood intersects with someone who's a possible terrorist or a criminal, okay, all of a sudden, you may become a person of interest because of your intersecting networks . . . and all of a sudden you now get pulled into that sphere.

Does my intersecting network with someone else mean that we are both involved in criminal activity, or simply that we are both connected to some of the same people, or that we are connected through our mutual love of *The Wire*, rather than our mutual love of robbing hardware stores?

As we rush to embrace the power of data, then, we need to slow down, take a deep breath, and remember that data isn't a universal Magic Eight Ball designed to turn up all the answers. These are early days, and lots of research is being done into how to manage ad hoc, on-the-fly, continually self-generated data.

## LIFE IN THE DATA-MAPPED CITY

Charles Baudelaire wrote about the *flâneur*, the person who strolls the streets of the modern city without a goal beyond discovering the world around him, a "botanist of the sidewalk," as he described it. The city that is mapped and known so thoroughly is at odds with our notion of a mysterious, organic urban jungle waiting to be discovered. The truth is, though, we human beings are predictable creatures. Dull, but apparently true. Network scientist Albert-László Barabási, for instance, turned up extraordinary evidence of our predictability in research on cellphone users' behaviour. Based on data about where study participants had been (gathered from their phones), Barabási and his team were able to predict where subjects *would be* with an average of 93 per cent predictability; as he puts it, "only 7 percent of the time a person's whereabouts were a mystery."[16] If data shows where you've been, in other words, it also shows where you will go. This startling finding suggests the power of the information contained in the Data Map, but also the spooky fragility of our privacy in a data-mapped world.

The smart cities of the future will have lots of different types of data that will help us do everything from finding restaurants we like in new neighbourhoods, to helping plan traffic routes and improving public health outcomes. The challenge is to make all this information accurate and, more importantly, meaningful, and to do so in a way that respects individual privacy. The greatest danger, however, lies in not understanding that data is political. It's political in the sense that what we choose to gather and display says a lot about what we value and what we choose to ignore, much as those *mappae mundi* show what medieval people valued. It's also political in terms of who gets access to the data. I would like to think that data is not just for officials – governments, researchers, urban planners – but for us, the people who create the data, just as we create our city in the way we choose to inhabit it. You can view the city as built by governments or by corporations, or you can view it as built by citizens. Proponents of the open data movement push for just this sort of democratization of data. That democratization of big data sets is exciting, certainly, but we need to consider the warnings of people like Lawrence Lessig and Valdis Krebs. If data, and how we choose to correlate it, contextualize and recontextualize it, is braided with the subjective story of how we see the world around us, the risks are that we use the persuasive power of numbers – never mind all those lovely graphs – as ideological tools. (If I had known how powerful all this data would prove to be, I would have paid closer attention in math class.)

As I've suggested, for individuals, self-tracking can sometimes have an objectifying character, as we turn ourselves into productive machines of self-improvement. From a social point of view, I wonder what it means to understand the humans who use the city as variables in the system, rather than as citizens for whom the city is created, and who in turn create the city. If the smart city is about quickly responding to changing data, do we, in a sense, become a part of the technological system that is the city? We manage and regulate the city; we manage and regulate the self. If, at a micro level, we understand the power of self-tracking as a way to make ourselves more productive, healthy, and useful, at a macro level, do we risk thinking of ourselves as productive inputs for the health and wealth of the city? The history of treating people as a source of production for the whole doesn't have a very good track record. You don't have to have a particularly dystopian turn of mind to find that possibility tinged with a Foucauldian sense of a productive, managed, compliant society. These are the kinds of political assumptions about what data ought to be used for that we need to be alive to. All that data exhaust, all that self-reportage, all the preferences and check-ins, cries out for a new way of thinking about our informational ecosystem: a new politics of data.

[ EIGHT ]

# UNITE!
### You Have Nothing to Lose But Your
### Terms-of-Service Contract!

The Data Map is about more than merely the proliferation of stats. It's a sea change. We've never before had the ability to gather and analyze this sort of raw information about our own behaviour as individuals, or about our collective behaviour as citizens. In this new "ecosystem of information," behaviour is potentially radically transparent. Where once we could assume "privacy through obscurity" – that most of our behaviours were private simply because to monitor where people went and what they did would require an army of spies – in an increasingly digital world, that monitoring is becoming automatic and obscurity is lost. Monitoring is easy, in fact, especially since we are so willing to track ourselves. Just as we need to decide how we want to use this information in our own personal lives, so that we can harness its power without slipping into neurotic compulsion, we need to decide what rules govern this new world at a societal level. History shows us the paroxysms – revolutions, even – that accompany new information regimes. Think of the shakeup of the old notions of traditional authority that accompanied Gutenberg's moveable type – the print revolution brought with it new ways of thinking about who could produce and consume information, and who owned it. Any system of information has norms that govern how it functions: who controls it, how it's protected, what its appropriate uses are. We take those norms for granted; we think of them as moral laws, or as "natural." It's only when we're in the midst of the dawn of a new information ecosystem, as we are now, that we're vividly aware that, in fact, the rules governing it are up for grabs. You can see this today in our own battles over copyright, piracy, and intellectual property. The ease of replicating and sharing virtual goods such as music, movies, and e-books throws norms surrounding the ownership of information into question.

As a culture, we have been caught off-guard by the way this data boom has taken off, largely because it's happened quickly, and in a piecemeal fashion. We haven't had the time to address what our relationship to the data we're generating ought to be. The streams of data we're creating are worth something. We want to access the data for our own purposes, but it's also potentially useful to governments and to researchers interested in creating smarter policies and more responsive cities, and of course to the businesses with which we store that information. Our data helps companies track their customer base and sell targeted advertising to us. Data is becoming a new currency, and we didn't even see it coming.

What rules ought to govern this new information ecosystem? Who owns the data we're producing, and under what conditions? How can we structure the uses of the Data Map for our own and society's benefit while still protecting our privacy? This boom in data is, in equal measure, both valuable and fraught with pitfalls. If we're going to use it wisely, we need to wrestle with the two big questions that haunt digital culture: privacy and ownership. We need to balance the business models of companies using our data, the social value of information, and most importantly, our rights. The time to talk about this is now. Businesses that manage our data need to be transparent about how we manage what can be seen about us, what we can do with our data, and most importantly, what they can do with our data. The answers will come from legal tussles, research scholarship, and corporate boardroom battles. They also need to come from us. We may not be experts, but the data is ours. At the personal and the collective level, we are agents in handling our data and can use it for what it's good for, while avoiding the dangers.

## TEMPEST IN A FACEBOOK

When it comes to issues of privacy, personal data, and what corporations owe the users of their (mostly free) services, Facebook tends to be a flashpoint. Other Web 2.0 services have been dinged on issues of privacy, to be sure. Facebook, though, has so many people's personal data that its decisions are highly publicized. It's also the case that things like privacy settings and what information is publicly shared – and how – seem to change frequently. At times, Facebook has been perceived as almost cavalier in its approach to users' privacy. After a controversial set of changes to its privacy settings in 2010, for example, technology journalists and commentators asserted variously that Facebook had "gone rogue"[1] or that Facebook CEO Mark Zuckerberg was "overplaying his hand."[2]

And yet even the behemoth Facebook has ultimately had to pay attention to user concerns about privacy. If we're headed into a future of ever more self-tracking and personal data generation – and storing it in for-profit companies – we need to be aware of the role we can play as savvy consumers in shaping the policies that govern the companies we deal with. A platform for data collection is worthless without people willing to contribute their data. When we look at social networking services right now, we're looking at an embryonic form of the Data Map. We are already having extensive debates over issues such as privacy, security, ownership, or the improper use of people's data when it comes to how we use these services. How much more complex and intense will these debates be when we're not just talking about a couple of hundred tweets or status updates, but, in fact, the statistical representation of our lives?

When it comes to privacy concerns, people will often argue, essentially, *caveat Facebooker*. If you put your data online, you better be prepared for it to be public, the thinking goes. I myself have trotted out the old "don't post anything you wouldn't want to see on the front page of the newspaper" argument. While it's prudent to assume anything you post online is potentially public, it's an unnecessarily limiting way of thinking about protection of privacy.

Of course, you and I have a responsibility to figure out what we're comfortable with in terms of sharing information. We need to recognize that while we can always add to our data later, it's much more difficult to take it back (as many an oversharing teenager has learned). That said, companies have a responsibility to be stable and transparent about how they are managing data. It's not good enough to say that the tools are there for people to manage their privacy. This is not just a problem for newbie older users or teenagers. One study at Columbia University surveyed sixty-five students (presumably people who might be assumed to be pretty familiar with social networking and the online world). They found that while students cared about what sort of information was shared with whom, and intended to manage their privacy settings to reflect this, 93 per cent of them were inadvertently sharing something they didn't want others to see.[3] If a service is designed so that users who are interested in managing their data are not easily able to do so, it has been designed at best, poorly, and at worst, unethically.

These are private corporations, rather than governments, and our relationship with them is governed by the terms-of-service agreement we sign. As consumers, though, and more importantly, as agents who are actively shaping the new data ecosystem through our actions, we need to insist on corporate respect for the integrity and importance of our data. Many consumers already choose where to spend their money based on considerations like sustainability or corporate social responsibility. Why not also make such decisions based on a company's corporate data responsibility? While housing personal conversations, video and photo collections, lists of friends and contacts within one large organization such as Facebook is convenient, the degree of power it confers on a single company – a company with an active interest in collecting as much of our data as possible – is troubling. If nothing else, Facebook's dominance illustrates the dangers of what's called the "network effect." The more people who use Facebook, the more useful it becomes to all the people using it. The converse of this is that no matter how unhappy you might be with how Facebook deals with your privacy, leaving Facebook starts to feel like pushing yourself out to sea on a solitary life raft, and waving goodbye to the populated cruise ship having a party on board. If nothing else, the emergence of a competitor such as Google Plus is good for this reason.

## DESIGN AND YOUR DATA

In the spring of 2010, four young New York University computer science students decided they would create a new social networking service, one based on giving the users greater control over their data. It was to be called Diaspora. Hopes were high in the early going. They surpassed their initial funding drive by leaps and bounds on the crowd-sourced funding site Kickstarter. The germ of the Diaspora idea offered an intriguing alternative. Diaspora was supposed to make it easy for people to share information with those they wanted to, and not with those they didn't. They also wanted to make it clear that users owned their own data and could take it with them. More importantly, they reasoned that there was no need to have a central hub, which stored all the information users contributed and accessed, in the way Google Plus or Facebook stores users' data on its own servers. What if you allowed people to share information but also to store the data themselves?

The students behind Diaspora set about building a network that would challenge the assumption that she who creates the sandbox gets to keep all the pails and shovels. In the Diaspora model, the social network was supposed to be distributed in "pods." Essentially, as a user, you would have your own server, which hosts your data. Like any other social network, you use it to relate to other people, and to post information about yourself and others. The difference is that since you are hosting your information, you can be sure that you are maintaining greater control over your data. In an effort to make Diaspora work for people who found the idea of setting up their own home server a non-starting head-scratcher, the service also allowed users to join seeds hosted on other individuals' servers, or those of organizations such as universities. Users could also choose to store their data with Diaspora's own pod. This way, a user could at least participate in the social network, helping to avoid the "network effect" problem of a service that might only appeal to data activists and the tech-savvy.

At time of writing, Diaspora is still in early (alpha) development and it remains to be seen whether the service will take off. Tragically, one of its young founders died in the fall of 2011. But the Diaspora case is important because it's a good example of how the decisions designers make affect the way the technology gets used down the road. The design decisions made by many of the companies that facilitate the kind of personal data generation we've been talking about are informed by a set of suppositions about where data ought to be stored. Once those design decisions are entrenched as the norm, it's hard to see that it might be any other way, and that what may seem natural – that a company should store the information that we create about our own lives and use it – is not natural. It's a design decision and a business decision. Diaspora and its "take your marbles and go home" approach, while an elegant solution, isn't one designed with profit top of mind. Companies that want to make money off your data have an inherent interest in keeping it in-house.

### DATA PORTABILITY: ON PICKING UP YOUR MARBLES AND GOING HOME

The ability to take your data with you easily (or not) is one of those design and business decisions. It's key to what the folks behind Diaspora have in mind, but it's also a much broader movement. Data portability means, as one definition has it, "the free flow of people's personal information across the Internet, within their control."[4] It doesn't just mean that I can pull down my data from a site when I choose to (although it does include that power), but also that the technical protocols exist so that I can easily move all of my information from one service to another. As of this writing, Facebook allows me to download my data to the hard drive of my computer, so that the record of all those wall posts and photo albums can exist outside of the world of Facebook.

That's a good thing. The exception is that it doesn't allow me to download my contacts' email addresses, unless I have their specific permission. Of course, having my contacts without a way of reaching them outside of Facebook limits the usefulness of that information and reveals some of the thorny issues around storing personally valuable information with a third-party service. (Facebook has argued that giving up contacts would be an impingement on the other users' privacy.)

Data portability sounds like a principle only a geek could love, but it's important for a couple of reasons. One is that regardless of where I happen to be storing my data, the data belongs to me, and I ought to be able to take it with me, to do what I want with it, including moving it to another service. This is a relatively trivial issue for most of us now, because most people's contribution of data is limited to something like a Twitter feed, or a Flickr account, or a LinkedIn profile. In the world of the Data Map, however, you will be producing volumes of data, possibly spread across a great many private and public data storage services. You will need to be the bearer of your data, and for it to be used effectively, you will need to get at it, move it, and recontextualize it in ways that suit your needs. When I spoke to Nicholas Felton, he was frustrated that he couldn't import data collected from one service into Daytum to use it for the kind of analytics he wanted to use it for:

> We're working to connect it [Daytum] to these myriad services that are out there now . . . we're interested in giving people the tools to tie, say, their Netflix account to the weather or whatever they want. There are a lot of one-off services that,

say, "measure your productivity" . . . we'll use our metrics to tell you how productive you are, but I think for everyone it's a different story. Maybe you're affected by the weather and maybe you're not, but if you have access to all these different data sources and data streams, I think it would be nice to give people the tools to really analyze them and make the funny or serious associations that they think are important to them.

Elias Bizannes of the DataPortability Project has argued for data portability by drawing an analogy to the financial system, which allows us to move our funds amongst banking institutions or different types of services.[5] Indeed, it's unimaginable to suggest that a bank, say, would tell you that you can't move a chunk of your funds from institution A to a mortgage held at institution B. Why should data be any different? He further suggests that this may benefit the online companies too, since they will have access to an updated, accurate picture of your information, as long as you choose to maintain a relationship with them.

We could, then, think of our data as something like our money, something we own by virtue of having generated it. We might also think of it as a part of who we are as people, in the same way we think of our I.D. as a representation or documentation of who we are as individuals. The data we generate is then seen as a persistent, portable part of personal identity. That doesn't mean we can't negotiate to store it, or loan it, in exchange for a service we like. We enter into these sorts of data agreements all the time already. When we use loyalty cards, we (ought to) understand that we are giving up our data in exchange for bargains down the road.

## DESIGN FOR ANONYMITY:
## CAN DATA BE BOTH USEFUL AND ANONYMOUS?

Let's say that one of the rules of governance in this new information ecosystem will be that our data must be portable, because it is a part of our identity that we should be able to take with us wherever we wish. It must be able to move from platform to platform fluidly so that as individuals we can make use of it the way we want. Let's further assume, since we're the ones creating the rules for this new world, that privacy settings will be transparent, so that each of us can be clear on what we're sharing with whom. We should be able to make effective use of our data as individuals, correlating it, observing it over time, making use of it to improve our health outcomes, manage our finances, or set goals for ourselves.

What of the power of our information in the aggregate? What rules will we need to set in place so that the information we're generating collectively can be just as useful? If our new ecosystem is to provide us with useful information as a society, it must also protect the identity of individuals providing it. People who deal in large data sets often speak casually of "anonymizing" data to protect individuals' identity, but this, it turns out, is a tricky business indeed.

It sounds simple enough: just remove personally identifying information, and aggregate. No one needs to know that "Nora Young" takes the 9:15 bus to midtown every morning, or that she missed her bus on May 9 because she slept badly the night before after eating twelve pickled onions, all data I might well be recording for my personal benefit – they only need to know aggregate numbers of people taking the 9:15 bus, and perhaps where they are coming from. In the research world, we have some pretty good examples of how accessing anonymous data has worked. According to Francesco Calabrese, the researcher I spoke to at MIT's SENSEable City Lab, the telecoms they have dealt with are, for instance, bound by tight regulations on how cellphone user data can be used, and of course, individual user identities are not relevant to the work the Lab does. Telecommunications, though, is a tightly regulated industry, and access to data is confined to respected academic research. In the more casual world of start-ups and publicly accessible data, the record is more troubling, even where individually identifying information has been removed.

One of the most high-profile examples of the tricky business of anonymity involved the online movie rental service Netflix. Based on the record of movies a subscriber watches, Netflix makes recommendations, much in the way Amazon does with books. The recommendations are more accurate if subscribers also rate the movies they've seen, and user ratings are part of what makes the recommendation system "smart." Back in 2006, Netflix launched a contest called the Netflix Prize. It was an exercise in crowdsourcing, to see if someone outside of the company could come up with a more accurate algorithm for recommending movies than the one Netflix was using at the time; the one-million-dollar prize guaranteed it would be a high-profile contest. As *Wired* magazine described it,[6] Netflix released information about the movies subscribers rented and the reviews of those movies that subscribers had submitted. In the enormous data set Netflix released, subscribers were identified only by a unique ID number, not by name.

Without knowing the names and addresses of the Netflix users in question, researchers from the University of Texas were able to identify some (though certainly far from all) Netflix customers from the data sets, including potentially sensitive information such as sexual and political orientation, by correlating the data with information some users posted (under their own names) to an outside source, the Internet Movie Database. As the researchers themselves described it, "We demonstrate that an adversary who knows only a little bit about an individual subscriber can easily identify his or her record if it is present in the dataset, or, at the very least, identify a small set of records which include the subscriber's record."[7] One woman – a lesbian who was not publicly out about her sexuality – filed a lawsuit over the issue, on the basis that the data hadn't been made sufficiently anonymous (the suit was subsequently settled).

The Netflix case highlights several serious risks associated with releasing even aggregate, anonymized data. First, the data sets were released to more than 50,000 prize contestants. It's not as though you can just ask everyone to put their heads down on their desks and hand over the information without looking at it. Who knows how many people might potentially see the information, and what might happen to it down the road, once it's out in the wild? Second, the data left identifying trails *because users chose to self-track their movie preferences*. It's not just that people whose identities were exposed were using the service, in the way that we all risk cracked passwords and hacked accounts. They were identifiable precisely because they had developed a useful feedback loop with the Netflix site, as well as created public ratings of their movie preferences at another site. They had provided customer ratings, which both improved the recommendations that were made to them and allowed Netflix to make more accurate recommendations to other users with similar tastes, thus improving the service overall. In short, it's a perfect example of the way auto-reporting can be used effectively. Unfortunately, it's also an example of how this can go wrong. If there was not enough information to identify (some) people in the Netflix data set itself, there was when it was correlated with another data set. On Netflix's part, there was no sinister abuse of people's right to privacy. However, there was an error in assessing what risks there might be to users' privacy.

The Netflix case is a good example of what I mean about the Data Map catching us unawares. I'm sure the vast majority of Netflix customers don't think of themselves as self-trackers who need to make decisions about what to track or how or about whom they wish to share it with. They're simply people who want a convenient way to watch movies; however, their convenient method also leaves a digital trail; when it's combined with other self-tracking behaviour (here, recording their reactions to movies) and made public, even seemingly anonymous data is potentially leaky. What's most chilling about the Netflix example is that identification was possible even though the University of Texas researchers only had access to two sources of self-tracking information, Netflix and Internet Movie Database. What sorts of links will people be able to make once much, much more of our everyday behaviour is tracked and recorded?

Arvind Narayanan and Vitaly Shmatikov are the researchers at the University of Texas at Austin who de-anonymized the Netflix data, and it's not an isolated case of less-than-anonymous anonymized data. Besides their work on the Netflix case, they have also demonstrated the ability to de-anonymize social networks, using a roughly similar technique of taking one data set and correlating it with another. If you don't think you have anything to worry about in terms of privacy, sit up. In one study, they demonstrated that "a third of the users who are verifiable members of both Flickr and Twitter can be recognized in the completely anonymous Twitter graph with only 12% error rate, even though the overlap in the relationships for these members is less than 15%!"[8]

Sharing and aggregating information is essential if the Data Map is going to be useful, but clearly, we need a lot more research to understand what constitutes safe sharing of information, particularly since the tools for crunching and correlating that data are only going to get stronger. While in the vast majority of cases the information is valuable precisely for what it reveals in the aggregate, rather than by knowing who individuals are, Naryanan and Shmatikov's research reveals disturbing holes in secure data management.

## THERE OUGHTTA BE A LAW!

As a technology journalist, I sign up for a lot of online services; I mean, a lot, as I go about researching the latest developments online. Sometimes, I feel as though bits and pieces of me are scattered across the Web. I don't know that

I've ever read a terms-of-service agreement through to the end, and when I have explored the terms of service, it's usually very difficult to understand basic things like what a business actually plans to do with my data, how long they are going to keep it, and so forth. Like most people, I unthinkingly tick the box that says I've read and understood the terms, and away we go.

As we see from the Netflix example, what other parties – specifically the companies that I store my data with – can do with my information is at least as important as how I choose to manage my own information. I wanted to know if there was a more robust way to protect my data than ticking "I agree" to a document I barely understand, so I contacted Ian Kerr, Canada Research Chair in Ethics, Law, and Technology at the University of Ottawa. Kerr is a leading expert in issues of anonymity and privacy in the digital, networked era. He told me that there are two relevant areas of the law when it comes to those terms-of-service agreements we unthinkingly accept: intellectual property and contract law. The issue at stake comes down to striking a balance between consumer protection and freedom of contract. The terms-of-service agreement we all click "yes" to is something called a standard form agreement. I don't go back and forth negotiating a specific contract between Nora Young and Facebook before I sign up, for obvious reasons; everyone who signs up for Facebook agrees to the same boilerplate contract. The challenge, as Kerr describes it, is that so far the courts have tended to privilege the standard form agreement in that balancing act, because users agreed to the terms of service, even in cases where, from a practical point of view, it's hard to see how consumers were informed in a meaningful way. Kerr told me about a high-profile case a number of years ago involving a major Internet and cable provider. The company wanted to change the terms of service of its contract, but didn't send out notices to its customers. Instead, they posted the changes to their website. When it came before the courts, the service provider's argument was that, as Kerr explains, "the initial contract said when it comes to notice, we reserve the right to do it one of three ways: we'll send you a notice, we'll phone you, or we'll post it on our website. And so because it was in there, the courts basically said, Well, you had the ability to look at that."

From Kerr's point of view, the problem with resting so much power in a terms-of-service contract is that it essentially allows companies to do an end run around privacy considerations. "You have the privacy protection in the statute, and then because they make you sign the contract, you basically waive those privacy rights, whereas it seems to me the question from the outset is whether you actually truly consented to that contract, but the threshold of contract is extremely low."

As we head into a world where more and more of our data is posted online, we need to challenge this disturbing pattern. Even from the point of view of intellectual property, the strength of those ill-understood contracts can allow companies to claw back data that common sense would dictate users should own. We are filling the Web with images, opinions, tastes, and preferences; whose intellectual property ought that to be, if not our own? The law is notoriously slow when it comes to responding to technological change. If we are, however, at the dawn of a new information ecosystem, where personal data has a volume and a value unprecedented in history, we ought to be thinking differently about the sorts of contracts ordinary citizens sign with online companies. Kerr's vision is to establish parameters on what's acceptable in those standard agreements.

Variations on privacy tussles are taking place all over the world, as Web 2.0 companies with millions of international users come into conflict with various jurisdictions' privacy laws. The European Union began revising its privacy laws in late 2010, to update the existing 1995 (pre–Web 2.0) data protection rules, and has more recently been adamant that transnational companies such as Facebook need to comply with EU regulations if they are to operate there.[9] Canada has been working out what a more reasonable idea of informed consent might look like, through the Office of the Privacy Commissioner and PIPEDA, the Personal Information Protection and Electronic Documents Act. One of the keys to the Canadian approach is that user consent needs to be *meaningful*, such that the user understands "the purposes for collecting, using, and disclosing personal information."[10]

### PROTECTING DATA TO SAVE THE DATA MAP

To achieve personal data security, we need rules of data use that are transparent and that comply with legal norms in different jurisdictions. It would be better yet if privacy regimes could have international heft, such as the EU is doing. However, we still want to be able to make use of that information as a society. Those researchers who imagine using the Data Map for the kinds of public benefits we have discussed obviously have an interest in accessing data, but they are also interested in establishing a regime where personal privacy can be respected. Nathan Eagle, whose research focuses on predicting human behaviour by observing how people move about with their cellphones, took on the problem of anonymity in a paper he delivered at the Engaging Data conference at MIT in 2009.[11] He acknowledged the problem of "deductive disclosure," essentially the problem Narayanan and Shmatikov identified in their work in the Netflix case. Eagle argued that researchers ought to adhere to strict protocols, such as storing the original data on a secure computer that doesn't have Internet access, using more "rigorous anonymization techniques," and limiting the length of time researchers can access data. It's an excellent suggestion as far as it goes but, as we've seen, the urge to use aggregated data for insight – and for business – extends way beyond the academy. I imagine data being used in academic research, certainly, but also by urban planners, public health officials, community groups, business, and more.

MIT's Alex Pentland has argued that we need a "new deal on data."[12] He suggests in an essay that we need to think about balancing the ability to use data for public good with respecting the rights of the individual. Pentland envisions handing over to individuals the ownership of their personal data, and ownership would include the right to remove all one's data from a company at any time. The individual would be the one ultimately in control.[13]

One can imagine this sort of data ownership model being used in tandem with Ian Kerr's stricter set of limits on the sorts of provisions that can be put into terms-of-service contracts in the first place, so that the user cannot be made to sign away his right to own, move, and dispose of his data in any way he wishes.

At our meeting, I asked Kerr where he thought the debates around personal data and the law were heading. He noted that in the legal history of personal information privacy, the battle so far has been about what rules ought to govern collection of data, and that the future may well lie in what we can do with our personal data *after* it's been collected. He then speculated that

> we're going to need norms that say *even if* you have access to that information because you provide the platform or because you're a third party that that platform shares it with, or because someone took [that information] and posted onto the Internet – however it got disclosed, we might still have norms and rules about its use.

In short, no matter how information was disclosed, we still need rules that govern what a company can do with an individual's information, and these restrictions ought not to be the sort of thing that a user waives in a terms-of-service agreement.

These scenarios are not merely speculative, either. It's already the case, for instance, that life insurance companies take into account the publicly accessible information you leave behind. In one well-publicized case in Quebec, a woman had her long-term disability benefits cancelled owing to posts she had made on Facebook. She was on leave for depression, but the insurance company used images she had posted of herself on a sun vacation as evidence that she was no longer depressed.[14] Insurance companies are using the data we voluntarily post about ourselves proactively, as well. According to The Wall Street Journal,[15] data collection businesses look for information such as fan pages on social-networking sites to get an idea of overall lifestyle and health risks of prospective policy holders. Tomorrow's self-trackers might be willing to share their data-mapped health profile with insurance companies or agree to participate in this sort of continual health monitoring in exchange for lower premiums, but should insurance companies be allowed to snoop into our self-tracking data on their own, or purchase that data from third parties, and offer differential pricing according to what they think that data shows?

An intriguing proposition has come up amongst a handful of influential legal scholars in the United States, such as Daniel Solove, Lawrence Lessig, and Jonathan Zittrain, with respect to this idea of use. Solove suggests copyright law might offer something of a model.[16] In copyright law, information flows and can be legitimately displayed or copied (or both) in certain contexts, he argues, but not in others. There's a range of acceptable uses. Treating my data as a form of intellectual property with a flexible system of when and how it can be used certainly opens up a lot of room for fruitful discussion. The copyright system works to accomplish a few things: to protect the rights of the holder of copyright, to indicate where there are rights of use for you and me, and more broadly, to encourage innovation. It accepts that there is a public, social good not in unfettered access, but in balancing collective rights, social good, and individual protection, and this understanding may prove a helpful model for protecting data.

To add to the already daunting list of ownership and regulation questions I've sketched out here, we'll also need to think about who controls the information generated by all the devices in our lives that are accumulating data about us. As we've explored, the Data Map consists not only of the information I choose to track about my behaviour but also passive data that's been collected by digital technology. From my perspective, I believe that I ought to be able to access the data, for example, that my phone collects about where I am when I use it, even if that information is also required for the effective operation of the phone. However, this access is not the way things are shaping up in the early going, as companies make use of the information we contribute about our habits. The Internet-dependent services we use to watch movies, to listen to music, and to read books, for instance, collect a lot of information about how we are using them. US author and researcher Simson L. Garfinkel has argued in *Technology Review* magazine that this is part of the character of content when it is accessed through cloud computing services, such that "previously inanimate possessions can now talk about you behind your back."[17] He raises the prospect of a future in which that data may be used not just to improve the service you get but also for the interests of third parties:

Apple could combine its own data with commercial data banks to tell Beyoncé the number of men aged 25 to 30 who are buying her tunes in New York City, for example; the music you place in Google's cloud storage and playback service could shape the advertising that you see all over the Web.[18]

But of course the rules for who can do what with your data, and under what conditions, are going to become more complicated still. Increasingly, the data that's collected about how we move through our environment won't be in devices that we own. Just as the subway turnstile does not require our consent to tote up the fact that another body has passed through it, or the closed circuit cameras that fill downtown streets and stores don't require our consent to record us, our environments are increasingly filled with sensors that passively gather information about citizens. As Ian Kerr explained it to me, conventional notions of meaningful consent don't really make sense when we're talking about technologies in our environment collecting data "in the background." He suggests that we'll need a separate set of rules that govern what can be done with information in situations where meaningful consent isn't feasible.

Clearly, there are issues around data ownership, meaningful consent, and the collective good that need to be wrangled in our new information ecosystem. It's daunting, mostly because the systems we have in place around contracts and consent and rights are really designed for an analog era, an older information ecosystem. As the lines of The Data Map are being drawn, we need to think beyond a debate between corporate interest versus individual privacy.

How might we start to regulate this relationship, which is now governed by the whims of terms-of-service contracts, and see it more as an integrated relationship between governments, private corporations, researchers, and individuals? Alex Pentland has argued that his "new deal on data" needs to be taken on in tandem with encouraging the use of our data for the common good.[19] Perhaps it's a new deal, or perhaps it's a new legal framework. I think that the key to encouraging us not only to protect our privacy but also to use it for public good lies in thinking of ourselves as curators and agents of our own data. Yes, our data is personal, but in another sense it's social. We don't live as isolated atoms. The pattern of our movement is connected to how others are moving, and to our relationship to them. The answers to regulation and protection of this data will lie with lawyers, governments, and privacy scholars, but we also need to step up. The new world of the Data Map requires a new world of Data Activists.

# NINE

# THE DATA MAP AND YOUR FUTURE
## Becoming a Data Activist

In the space of a few years, self-tracking has gone from being a fringe activity to an increasingly ordinary part of daily life. It's almost effortless to fold personal note-taking into our day's routine, and getting easier all the time. We've seen how the growth of portable digital devices, from phones to e-readers, takes that tracking one step further, bringing tracking out into the world with us. Increasingly, the default setting in our digital lives is to track information about ourselves, whether we make a conscious choice to do so or not. The last piece of the tracking puzzle, and the future of the Data Map, is the rise of the Internet of Things, which is shorthand for what happens when ordinary objects that we don't recognize as computers – your fridge, your shoes, the checkout at the supermarket, the bus stop on the corner – are equipped with small amounts of computing power and can communicate information to the Internet.

The Internet of Things is going to have a big impact on how people decide to self-track; in fact, it's already starting to. For instance, if you are monitoring your weight and body fat, you may already have BodyTrace, an Internet-enabled scale that automatically communicates your weight to the website of the same name. Future tracking applications of the Internet of Things might include, say, smart textiles that communicate information about your body in order to regulate the heating and cooling system of your home, or fridges that are aware of what is being consumed from them, or pill bottles that know when prescription medications have been taken.

More than that, the Internet of Things means that these computational objects will be networked to one another. You won't need to decide that you want to be on a diet and choose to take pictures of your food for your What I Ate blog if the fridge knows what food you've eaten, your scale knows your weight changes, and the fridge and scale can talk to each other. Perhaps your fridge will prompt you to eat broccoli when your body fat levels get a little on the high side. Hooray!

Beyond the use of sensors in the objects around us, though, in most visions of a fully networked, smart city, the humble cellphone will continue to play a key role. It can tell us incredibly useful information – where people are, what's going on around them – without the need for additional technology. Because of the near ubiquity of cellphones, the benefits of this smart city vision of the future aren't limited to the developed world, either. In the developing world, data (properly anonymized) from people's cellphones can provide more accurate information about less structured environments, such as urban slums, than a formal census might. In one current example, cellphone data was used to figure out where to build latrines in Rwanda[1]. The power of a dynamic Data Map lies not just in making the lives of the privileged more comfortable, or their weight easier to manage, but in making tangible, important benefits in people's lives and health the world over.

These three types of real-time data – active self-tracking, passive tracking through digital devices, and data captured via the Internet of Things – are coming together to create something truly new. We are looking ahead to a world where continually updated information about the city, and about how we are interacting with it, is ubiquitous, as fluid and available as electricity from a light switch or water from a tap. Given that a lot of the data in this new ecosystem is going to come from you, the question is, How do you want to live in a world like this? As a society, we want to harness the power of our data to build smarter, more responsive and sustainable environments without risking our privacy. To do so, we have to set aside our reflex to "tick the box to agree to the terms of service," blithely surrendering our data without demanding greater understanding of, and power over, where it goes. In this new information ecosystem, more can – and will – be known about us than ever before. We can choose to do nothing about it, or we can claim that data as our own and actively engage with how it's used.

This is a political issue but also a highly personal one. We need to take seriously the impact these technologies and practices can have on our relationship to our own bodies and to our sense of self. We can, if we are careful, use these tools consciously and thoughtfully to connect more deeply with ourselves, and with our bodies, rather than let ourselves drift in a relentless sea of numbers. Numbers can reveal things to us, but they don't tell the whole story. We need to weigh the numbers against the story that our own bodies, and our own hearts, are telling us. Collectively, and individually, then, we must become Data Activists.

## THE CUPCAKE MACHINE:
## THE DANGERS OF PERSONAL SELF-TRACKING

Some time after I settled on the image of a Data Map of the self as a way of thinking about the coming data boom and our participation in it, I came across someone who is literally making body maps from data. Paula Gardner is an associate professor in liberal studies at OCAD University in Toronto and co-director of the mobile experience lab there. In her ongoing project, called Biomapping, she's creating 2D and 3D maps based on people's biometrics. So, of course, I had to hotfoot it over to OCAD, to see what she was up to.

For her Biomapping project, Gardner gives regular people consumer-grade technologies for just the sort of personal monitoring we've been talking about in this book, based on their own ideas of the data they'd need to capture to create an accurate "map" of themselves. They use cellphones, as well as some higher-end technologies. For instance, there are now consumer devices developed for gaming applications that track alpha, beta, and theta waves in the brain. The volunteer participants gather data and, once it's recorded, they figure out how they want that data to be organized, in order to process the large amounts of raw data into a useable form. Finally, the idea is that they can create their own visualizations – their own maps – of themselves. It might be a two-dimensional map or, better yet, a three-dimensional object printed out from the university's own 3D printer. A 3D printer is a technology that's used to create three-dimensional prototypes. Essentially, it spits out layer upon layer of material – it might be a plastic of some sort, or a corn-based material, though in Paula's case, it's plasticine – until it builds up a 3D version of a design. Paula tells me they sometimes call their printer the Cupcake Machine, because it prints out objects about the size of a cupcake. What a perfect illustration of the objectified, data-mapped, self-tracked individual we've become: to be able to "print yourself out"! You could stick yourself up on the mantel alongside your golf trophy.

Paula's project, as you've probably guessed, is about critiquing the way we think about all this personal data we're producing, and what self-tracking really means in terms of the way we understand ourselves. We love to see an image of ourselves, in the same way we love to read our horoscope. Even if we know it's illusory, or even a bit ridiculous, we'll grasp at anything that seems to offer a concrete picture of ourselves; Paula's Biomapping has simply taken this to an extreme. It goes beyond that, though. Paula's project asks us to question what these monitoring tools really tell us and why we uncritically accept what they tell us. Her take is that a particular sort of "biomedical discourse" has been taken up in the culture, coming to us from psychiatric science in particular. In its popularized form, that discourse equates the self with the brain, and reduces the brain to what is computable. As she put it to me, the way this medicalized view of the self is simplified in popular culture suggests that "if you can know [the individual] through biomedical science or psychiatric science then your mood is computable; your personality is computable." The full richness of human personality is flattened, by reducing it to that which can be subjected to computation.

The biomedical self is precisely the sort of body that needs to be scrutinized for signs of ill health. This attitude toward our health, she thinks, doesn't just come to us from the pharmaceutical industry, but from consumer advocacy groups, and from public policy aimed at "healthy, productive populations." Paula talked to me about how she sees this playing out in biomedical technologies of self-tracking and health monitoring:

> Personal security hinges on mediating risk to the self, so risk is being expanded . . . We're encouraged to constantly mediate risk. It's sensible to us, it seems like it would make your parents glad! . . . It all fits very nicely into this idea of the appropriate consumer-citizen, and I think that's part of the reason why it's so hard to step back and look critically at "how am I making myself?"

This question of "how am I making myself?" is one we can ask ourselves with respect to self-tracking. That driven, hyperregulated image Paula points to is the danger that self-tracking taken to an extreme presents. It's a self that's been turned into an object, a machine, a functional tool. More than that, it's a self that's an "appropriate consumer-citizen." This perfectible view of the self is the latest point in a process that began with the evolution of the modern self. Remember philosopher Charles Taylor's idea of a "disengaged" subject, which emerged centuries ago? "The subject of disengaged and rational control," he writes, "has become a familiar modern figure. One might almost say it has become one way of construing ourselves, which we find hard to shake off."[2] It's a subject that engages in a kind of perpetual scrutiny, as Taylor describes it. The picture of the self that emerges is "the growing ideal of the human agent who is able to remake himself by methodical and disciplined actions."[3] And further,

what this calls for is the ability to take an instrumental stance to one's given properties, desires, inclinations, tendencies, habits of thought and feeling, so that they can be *worked on*, doing away with some and strengthening others, until one meets the desired specifications.[4]

Gee, that sounds familiar, doesn't it? That sense of relentless, driven perfectibility – examining the charts and graphs of the self's performance, spotting trends and noting lapses – is familiar territory in the world of self-tracking. It's the model of the productive, obedient self, such as the Nora who willingly submits herself to the chastising report of RescueTime. We internalize that performing, disciplined ideal, but in self-tracking, we turn the responsibility for creating that self over to digital technology that does the monitoring for us and presents us with the evidence of our success or failure. It's a strange twist on the idea of goal achievement and human agency. On the one hand, the goal of self-tracking is a kind of act of strength of will and agency, whether that's for the purpose of a "just do it" sense of improving yourself, or whether it's in the drive to a more transparent, full knowledge of the self. On the other, it involves a kind of submission to a system, which seems to deny the engagement of the subject. You don't even have to be aware enough of what's going on in your own skin to feel it, because the monitors will take care of it for you. This is a vision of the body and the self which is of a piece with under-standing yourself to be like a machine, a machine that needs to be ordered and maintained for optimal functioning. It's agency through submission.

Our idea of self is an inheritance of the modern era. We come by it honestly. It is also a response to the disembodi-ments of digital life. It is an attempt to tether the physical self, precisely because we are so often not "in" our bodies. We run, and map our runs, as if to assert and assure ourselves of our physicality, but in daily life, we do not "reside" in our bodies. We track what is knowable digitally and therefore lends itself to objective reportage. This view of the self is one that rewards observation and reportage more than analog introspection. We choose numbers and discrete, precise description, rather than wool-gathering, rumination, or lengthy text. And so I might suggest a distinctively twenty-first-century spin on this modern self: call it the Computational Self.

This way of seeing ourselves as *computational* is rampant in our culture. We routinely use the computer as a metaphor for human thought, even though we know that human memory doesn't work the same way computer memory does. We believe that we are knowable through objective, data-driven information. Of course, we can learn things about ourselves by gathering and reflecting on the data we produce. The problem is that the computational view of the self doesn't leave room for that which is not reducible to being computed. What becomes of what you can't document in data and stats? The computational view doesn't leave space for the fully embodied savouring of simple experience. It removes the place for the subjective narrative that we create for ourselves through introspection, and through abiding with others.

## ON BABY AND BATHWATER:
## I'M SURE THERE'S A MONITORING APP FOR THAT

While I do think there are real dangers in self-tracking, or at least in self-tracking run amok, I'm not arguing that we need to chuck out the pedometer and start the day with a plateful of French fries and mayonnaise. But when we look at any technology, and particularly any technology that works so directly on the body, we need to be alert to its hidden assumptions and biases. Technologies of measurement and monitoring carry with them a bias for a reduction to the statistical, and a bias toward "measuring up," performing, and regulation. We can, though, find a way that we can use these technologies to our advantage. We're not going to reinvent the bias of these technologies, and we're certainly not going to reinvent the building blocks of the modern Western idea of self, but we can question the social norms and business plans that under-lie how we are expected to use these technologies. The path to reclaiming technologies of self-tracking lies in reground-ing in the body, and in critical awareness. It is in this sense that we become activists in the use of our own data.

The parameters of the sort of data collected aren't natural, nor are they neutral. They are set largely by businesses with an interest in eliciting and sharing information in a particular way. It might seem obvious to list the music, movies, recre-ational activities, and TV shows you like on your Facebook profile, but aren't you about more than that? Who says you ought to list the commodities that you are interested in as a way of describing yourself? The use of lists and tags to link information is partly what digital technology privileges. It's also, though, what target marketing privileges. As we think about how to use data effectively, we have to question not just what's happening to our data, but what data is being col-lected in the first place. It's our choice where we choose to track our data, and we can choose our tools wisely.

A key way of choosing wisely is to think critically about the assumptions that are built into the design of these tools. Are they designed to give us the ability to decide what and how to track, in line with our own values, or are they designed purely for the production of obedient consumers and target markets? What I like about the Daytum.com platform I used in my year of self-tracking, for instance, is that it is so open-ended. It doesn't presume a social norm (losing weight, say) that it's "for." It allows me to articulate what and how I want to track. Design decisions may seem neutral but in fact imply a judgement. The Kindle, for instance, allows readers not only to learn what the most popular highlighted passages are in books, but also allows Kindle users to share the electronic notes they take while reading with others. This implies the judgement that we ought to be interested in reading the same way others are reading. Why should this be so? Maybe it is a good idea to know what other people are highlighting, and the notes they're making, but maybe we're sharing that information simply because the technology is good at doing that. Maybe we're being encouraged to share that information because making what was once a private experience into an online social activity run by a commercial entity means that you're less likely to ditch your Kindle and buy an iPad to read on instead. If the goal of these technologies is partly to give us insight into ourselves, we ought to think in a much more open-ended and critically minded way about what they are measuring and tracking.

It is in the outliers, the people who are taking self-tracking the furthest, where we can see how we might use self-tracking in this critically minded sense. Consider Carlos Rizo, the physician self-tracker, for instance. Intriguingly, and importantly, Paula Gardner's project has something in common with Carlos Rizo's understanding of how to use self-tracking effectively. In her project, Gardner deliberately asked volunteers to participate actively in choosing the tools that would track them, and in deciding what criteria they would use to represent themselves. She wanted them to ask themselves what they would like it to show, what it meant. From interviewing Carlos, I had the same feeling from him, that he wasn't passively accepting what data told him. He was thinking about what the data showed him and what he chose to track. He approached it as an experimental space, and then he used that experimental data to bring himself *back to himself*, to reground himself in the experience of his body. As such, he wasn't reducing himself to what was computable; he was using computation to awaken the sort of attentive, non-judgemental listening to the body that is a core aspect of knowing ourselves. For him, this assumed an almost spiritual dimension, bringing "body, mind and soul all together." "It's a game," he told me, "to help you learn more about yourself in ways you never expected, and it's not only about the numbers; it's about that other journey." Carlos sees self-tracking as being in the service of insight, and of more conscious living, not as an end in itself.

What resonated with me about Rizo's stance is that it's actually very yogic. It involves a technique that creates a space for non-judgemental bodily awareness and introspection. It facilitates turning inward and returning to the wisdom of the body, rather than simply pushing the self outwards, performing to an external ideal. I think it's precisely in connecting to the body in this listening, introspective way that we get beyond the limits of the Computational Self.

## DATA ACTIVISM AND THE GREATER GOOD

As much as we need to be critically minded when using these tools as individuals, we also need to think about the social implications of our data, because it's in the social space that this data is both useful and risky. Our personal data is political. We need to treat our data as a consumer-rights issue, sure, but also, as a fundamentally political issue. We need to ask questions now about how that information ought to be used, and, as we saw in the last chapter, what rules ought to govern that, before tracking and self-tracking becomes an unquestioned reality. It simply doesn't make sense to dig in our heels and say that we don't want any data recorded. First, it's already being recorded but, more centrally, collection of our data can be a powerful social good. If we are only thinking of it as a relationship between ourselves and the companies we deal with, we're missing the social dimension. A Data Map that offers us a feedback loop, that extends and increases our information, is hugely exciting. I want to live in a world with buildings that respond to how people use them, with public policy that understands where resources are needed in urban communities in the developing world, or where epidemiologists can understand the spread of disease more quickly. Understanding how people are behaving in a real-time context is hugely promising, too promising not to explore.

There are plenty of times when we will want to make our data accessible for its social benefit. You could argue that these large, privately gathered data sets should only be made available to research organizations and to governments, bound by strict rules about how the data can be used.[5] We already have models for the kind of tight privacy regulations that should give us confidence in the information we're making public. Here in Canada, for instance, Statistics Canada is bound by tight rules around safeguarding the security of citizens' data and has practices in place to avoid inadvertent data breaches. And yet that conservative approach coexists with an overall social movement toward greater openness and more access to data, so that the general public, who are, after all, the people who created the data, have access to it.

The open data movement argues for less, not more, of a top-down approach to data. In the U.K., the Free Our Data movement, headed up by the *Guardian* newspaper, has pushed for the release of taxpayer-funded statistics so that they may be more broadly used. Many municipal governments are getting on the open-data bandwagon, looking for ways to make civic information available in a form that will allow citizen coders to make apps and tools from it. In New York City, they have even appointed a chief digital officer to look at improving the exchange of digital information between the municipal government and its citizens. (Surely the creation of such a position in the first place is recognition that the relationship between politics, data, and citizen access is a powerful and growing issue.) When it comes to the personal data we are generating, there's a strong case to be made for accessibility too. If we are the ones generating so much data, why should it be locked up when it can be more useful for the collective, for bottom-up approaches? The cases I described of the Portland, Oregon, pipe-bomb detection or the on-the-ground Geiger-counter readings from ordinary Japanese citizens suggest there are huge opportunities in crowd-sourced data, and in making that data freely available for non-governmental bodies to build open platforms and apps that can make use of them.

While privacy is obviously important, what excites me is the potential for us to opt in to using our self-tracking data for the social good. Just like those Japanese citizens choosing to be activists in collecting radiation information and contributing that data to make a bigger picture, we can choose to sign up for self-tracking projects when we can see the social benefit of them. Imagine the potential to discover things about how we are behaving and what we are thinking by joining in this crowdsourced information gathering.

Each of us can be data activists in the project to build smarter cities and better communities. Wouldn't it be wonderful if we were more active participants in this process, if citizen engagement meant being a crowdsourcing cartographer of the Data Map? I don't think governments, researchers, or think tanks alone should be charged with deciding what we map or what "matters." We can map our communities, our neighbourhoods, and our lives according to the values we articulate. The tools are there for us to use if we will only claim them.

This is a startling implication of the bottom-up character of data today and in the future. We no longer need to rely on hierarchical authority to gather our data and tell us what it means or how it is to be used. Pachube, the open-source platform that those Japanese Geiger-counter readers used to aggregate and display radiation information, is built on just this premise: that regular citizens ought to be able to participate. Pachube's CEO and founder Usman Haque told me in an interview on Spark that what concerns him is a world where big companies control the Internet of Things. The threat is

a future where massive corporations are designing the way our environments are going to respond to us. The scary vision of the future is the smart home that's so smart that you can't even do any DIY on it. The light bulb goes out and you've got to call in a specialist.

Forestalling this threat is important not just to enable practical home repairs in the smart city but also because it's essentially about ensuring Data Democracy:

> What I'm trying to encourage, I hope, is the capacity . . . to be part of the process of building [data sets], of questioning the standards of evidence behind things like data collection in the smart city. At the moment the government [and organizations] are amassing data sets, often of public data, and I'd like to see members of the public making data. So, it's not just about making data public, but about the public making data.

Pachube and its founder are part of a movement toward a more democratic approach to data. This way of thinking is gaining steam as the pieces of the Data Map come together. This movement recognizes that it's not just that we as individuals might want to use data to improve our own lives, but that even the act of choosing what to monitor is political. Adam Greenfield is a leading figure in the push for more democratic approaches to creating smart cities. In an interview on Spark, he told me "the question isn't is this technology good or bad, or do I approve of it or disapprove of it, it's: what could it be used for and what are the specific ways in which a community is asked to decide about what the technology is there for and if it lives up to their expectations." We should be agents not only in collecting the data but also in deciding what we as a community value and, hence, want to measure. For Adam Greenfield, this includes an open approach to data: "We think that the citizens ought to have the same visibility onto that [smart city] information that the municipality does. . . . You ought to be able to see how the city is deploying its resources. After all, as a tax-payer, you're paying for them."[6] We should be agents not only in collecting the data but also in deciding what we as a community value and, hence, want to measure.

Right now, tools such as Pachube still require technical knowledge, but they are getting easier to use all the time. More than technical expertise, we need political commitment to using these tools for the collective good. In our personal use of self-tracking, we need to maintain the kind of critical self-awareness that people such as Carlos Rizo have; in our collective use of the Data Map, we need to keep that same critical engagement – to make data part of a democratic discussion, to politicize it.

Ultimately, the picture that emerges from the Data Map is not of us as isolated individuals, but of us as people who are always surrounded by a web of connections, people who are radically in community. When Valdis Krebs, for instance, creates his social network visualizations, the patterns that emerge tell us about the strength of the group and also about the strength of the individuals within the group. A social network is considered "brittle," that is, not functioning effectively, when it is not woven with many connections. It is vulnerable, because breaking one connection means setting the rest adrift. People in the network are effective to the extent that they are connected, in a multiplicity of ways, to others. In the same way that the Internet itself is robust because it has many different ways that information can be routed and redirected, so we are healthiest when we are part of a web of connections. Our functioning as humans, after all, is not due to isolation but to the web of interconnections we find ourselves in. Far from the isolated solitary individuals of modern liberal culture, we are indeed "live nodes on the network," to use Linda Stone's term. We are and always have been, but our web of interconnection is now more visible in a digital world, where our data reveals the patterns of our interconnections. We see the six degrees of separation on social networks. We observe how ideas arise, flow, and morph on Twitter. The modern "disengaged" singular individual Charles Taylor so evocatively describes turns out, instead, to be open, interconnected, webby.

When I asked self-tracker Carlos Rizo about his practice, he explained that tracking his personal health and the collective use of that information are intertwined for him:

> With what I've learned about myself, how can others benefit? It's that aspect of learning about myself but trying to give to others as well, because maybe by all sharing . . . we can, more at a philosophical level . . . [have] collective healing.

I think there's something profoundly true in the relationship between personal insight and the duty we have to others, and this is something to take into our approach to sharing data. After all, we create ourselves, choose what to value, to listen for and nurture, not as isolated individuals, but in community with others. Just as we can use self-tracking wisely to reconnect with the body on a personal level, on a social level, self-tracking and data collection can be tools to connect with what we truly value as a community. It can be an invitation to connect more deeply on a social and political level with those around us.

To use self-tracking effectively, we can't lose sight of the truth of embodied experience. The body is a source of knowledge – we learn about ourselves by being aware of our physical response to what is going on around us. When we attend to an experience with the intention of remembering, we create an opportunity for awareness, and self-awareness, which is missing if we are simply recording all the time. And we need to be open to the inchoate, to that which cannot be articulated in an objective manner or reduced to statistics.

Becoming data activists, agents in how we want to use data to make our real world, our bricks-and-mortar neighbourhoods and communities, better, is part of bringing ourselves back to ground, back to the truth of the physical.

[ ACKNOWLEDGEMENTS ]

One of the reasons I love making Spark is that it allows me to interview some of the finest minds creating and critiquing contemporary digital life. This book has been inspired and informed both by those conversations, and by the books these amazing people have written. My Spark colleagues have greatly influenced my journey through the book, in following their journalistic curiosity and passion, and in sharing mine. It's an amazingly talented team, and I'm very lucky to work with them. Linda Groen, director of current affairs at CBC Radio, has been very supportive of me and of Spark; my sincere thanks to her. CBC kindly agreed to let me quote from Spark interviews.

I am grateful to all the people I interviewed for this book. To a person, each was very generous with time and ideas. Any errors of interpretation are mine. It's been fascinating to see how the same themes and issues around technology, humanity, and social change crop up in different fields – from human computer interaction to history to art. Thanks in particular to the folks at MIT's SENSEable City Lab for facilitating my time there.

My friend Mark Morley read an earlier version of this book, and gave me invaluable help in thinking through some of the issues, and in clarifying terms and concepts in philosophy of technology. Mark is a true "technologian." I would also like to thank Sal Renshaw for her thought-provoking comments at an early stage. A number of the trends in this book, most notably medical monitoring, were first worked out in embryonic form with my good friend Cathi Bond, on our podcast, The Sniffer. My thanks to Cathi for allowing me my obsessions, and for the good-natured intellectual tussling.

My editor at McClelland & Stewart, Jenny Bradshaw, did an amazing job of shepherding me through the some-times nerve-wracking process of tackling a first book. Copy editor Lynn Schellenberg did a great job clarifying my writing. My agent, Chris Bucci at Anne McDermid & Associates, was tremendously helpful and a calming influence at crucial moments. Speaking of which, grateful thanks to Lisa Garber for keeping me on a (mostly!) even keel.

My grateful thanks to Rosanna Nardi for her unfailing support and patience during the writing of the book.

I've read a lot of books about yoga, and put together what I hope is an accurate – if abbreviated – take on a complex and varied philosophical system. My true knowledge of yoga has come from my teacher, Yogi Krishan Sidhu. Thank you for a lifetime of learning.

## INTRODUCTION

1. Nathan Eagle, "Engineering a Common Good: Fair Use of Aggregated, Anonymized Behavioral Data." Paper presented to Engaging Data Forum. MIT, Boston, October 12, 2009, available at http://senseable.mit.edu /engagingdata/program.html.

2. Nathan Yau and Jodi Schneider, "Self-Surveillance," ASIS&T Bulletin (June/July 2009), http://www.asis.org /Bulletin/Jun-09/JunJu109_Yau_Schneider.html.

## ONE

### AN ACCOUNTANT FOR THE BODY
*The Culture of Self-Tracking*

1. Gary Wolf, "The Data-Driven Life," New York Times, April 28, 2010, http://www.nytimes.com/2010/05/02 /magazine/02self-measurement-t.html.

2. "Are Metrics Blinding Our Perception?" by Anand Giriharadas, *New York Times*, November 20, 2009.
3. Foursquare.com, blog, January 24, 2011, http://blog.foursquare.com/2011/01/24/2010infographic/.
4. Mark McClusky, "The Nike Experiment: How the Shoe Giant Unleashed the Power of Personal Metrics," *Wired*, June 22, 2009, http://www.wired.com/medtech/health/magazine/17-07/lbnp_nike?currentPage=all.
5. Kate Murphy, "First Camera, Then Fork," *New York Times*, April 6, 2010, http://www.nytimes.com/2010/04/07/dining/07camera.html.
6. Andrew Knowlton, "3 Rules for Camera-Happy Diners (AKA Food Bloggers)," *Bon Appétit*, March 12, 2010, http://www.bonappetit.com/blogsandforums/blogs/bafoodist/2010/03/dear-ba-foodist-isnt-it.html.

TWO

## WE ARE ALL BEN FRANKLIN NOW
*Why We Self-Track*

1. Benjamin Franklin, *The Autobiography of Benjamin Franklin and Selections from His Other Writings*, introduction by Stacy Schiff (New York: Modern Library, 2001), 90.
2. Ibid., 94.
3. Ibid., 97.
4. Philippe Lejeune, *On Diary*, eds. Jeremy D. Popkin and Julie Rak (Honolulu: University of Hawaii Press, 2009), 53–55.
5. Ibid., 51.
6. Ibid., 58.
7. Ibid.
8. Ibid., 55.

9. Wolf, "The Data-Driven Life."
10. Thomas Goetz, *The Decision Tree: Taking Control of Your Health in the New Era of Personalized Medicine* (New York: Rodale, 2010).
11. Ibid., 70–93.
12. Lejeune, *On Diary*, 51.
13. Charles Taylor, *Sources of the Self: The Making of the Modern Identity* (Cambridge, MA: Harvard University Press: 1992), 175.
14. Ibid., 173.

THREE

## THOROUGHLY MODERN SELF-TRACKING

*Radically Shareable, Rearrangeable, Location-Specific Monitoring*

1. Wolf, "The Data-Driven Life."
2. "Over Five Billion Mobile Phone Connections Worldwide," July 9, 2010, BBC website, http://www.bbc.co.uk/news/10569081.
3. Summarized, for instance, in Derek Sivers's TED talk: http://www.ted.com/talks/derek_sivers_keep_your_goals_to_yourself.html.
4. Clive Thompson, "Brave New World of Digital Intimacy," *New York Times*, September 5, 2008, http://www.nytimes.com/2008/09/07/magazine/07awareness-t.html?pagewanted=1&_r=1.
5. Kathryn Zickuhr and Aaron Smith, "4% of Online Americans Use Location-Based Services," Pew Research Center, November 4, 2010, http://www.pewinternet.org/Reports/2010/Location-based-services.aspx.

FOUR

**THE DELIGHTS AND DAMAGE OF DIGITAL LIFE**
Self-Tracking as a Response to Losing the Ground Beneath Our Feet

1. Clay Shirky, Web 2.0 Expo SF 2008. "Gin and the Cognitive Surplus," April 25, 2008. Blip.tv, http://blip.tv /web2expo/web-2-0-expo-sf-2008-clay-shirky-862384.
2. For details on the Gin Craze, Ellse Skinner, "The Gin Craze: Drink, Crime & Women in 18th Century London," *Cultural Shifts*, November 2007, last modified January 28, 2008, see http://culturalshifts.com/archives/168.
3. Marshall McLuhan, *Understanding Media: The Extensions of Man* (Cambridge, MA: The MIT Press, 1994), 7.
4. Ibid., 57.
5. Ibid., 47.
6. Albert Borgmann, *Technology and the Character of Contemporary Life* (Chicago: University of Chicago Press, 1984).
7. Borgmann, "Focal Things and Practices," in *Technology and the Character of Contemporary Life* (Chicago: University of Chicago Press: 1984), 196–210.
8. Ibid., 197.
9. Ibid., 203.


FIVE

**MEET YOUR DIGITAL DOPPELGÄNGER**
The Future of the Data-Mapped Self

1. Yoav Gonen, "B'klyn Teacher Fakes Stair Fall to Avoid Review," *New York Post*, August 3, 2010, http://www.nypost.com/p/news/local/brooklyn /diving_instructor_LuCDC33xLo8e1oCiDLGVAL.

2. Abigail Sellen, Andrew Fogg, Mike Aitken, Steve Hodges,
   Carsten Rother, and Ken Wood, "Do Life-Logging
   Technologies Support Memory for the Past? An Experimental
   Study Using SenseCam," in *Proceedings of the ACM SIGCHI
   conference on Human factors in computing systems*, CHI'07,
   San Jose, California, 81–90.
3. Bell describes what he captured with the SenseCam as
   part of his book documenting his life-logging.
   C. Gordon Bell and Jim Gemmell, *Total Recall:
   How the E-Memory Revolution Will Change Everything*
   (New York: Dutton, 2009), 46–48.
4. Ibid., 81.
5. Ibid., 54.
6. Cory Doctorow, "My Blog, My Outboard Brain," O'Reilly
   Web Devcenter, May 31, 2002, http://oreilly.com/pub
   /a/javascript/2002/01/01/cory.html.
7. Bell and Gemmell, *Total Recall*, 23.
8. Jamais Cascio, "The Rise of the Participatory Panopticon,"
   Worldchanging.com, May 4, 2005, http://www.world
   changing.com/archives/002651.html.
9. As described in Brian X. Chen, "Why and How Apple Is
   Collecting Your iPhone Location Data," Wired.com,
   April 21, 2011, http://www.wired.com/gadgetlab/2011/04
   /apple-iphone-tracking/.
10. Viktor Mayer-Schönberger, *Delete: The Virtue of Forgetting in the
    Digital Age* (Princeton: Princeton University Press, 2009), 119.

SIX

**GOING SOCIAL**

*Your Data Map and the Coming Age of Big Data*

1.  Bill Hewitt, "Big Data: Big Costs, Big Risks and Big
    Opportunity," Forbes.com, May 27, 2011, http://blogs.forbes
    .com/ciocentral/2011/05/27/big-data-big-costs-big-risks-and
    -big-opportunity/.
2.  The "data deluge" is described in "Technology: The Data
    Deluge. Businesses, Governments and Society Are Only
    Starting to Tap Its Vast Potential." *The Economist*, February 25,
    2010, reprinted online at http://www.economist.com
    /node/15579717.
3.  Marshall Kirkpatrick, "Boom! Tweets & Maps Swarm to
    Pinpoint a Mysterious Explosion," *New York Times*, March 29,
    2010, http://www.nytimes.com/external/readwriteweb/2010
    /03/29/29readwriteweb-boom-tweets--maps-swarm-to
    -pinpoint-a-myste-34026.html?src=tptw.
4.  Mike Melanson, "From Calories to Sleep Cycles: What the
    Real-Time Web Means for Your Health," *New York Times*,
    June 8, 2010, http://www.readwriteweb.com/archives
    /from_calories_to_sleep_cycles_what_the_real-time
    _web_means_for_your_health.php.
5.  Steven Johnson, *The Ghost Map* (New York: Riverhead Books,
    2006), 222–226.
6.  Sarah Perez, "Tweeting Your iPhone Angst? AT&T Is
    Listening . . . On Twitter," *New York Times*/ReadWriteWeb,
    November 3, 2010, http://www.readwriteweb.com/archives
    /tweeting_your_iphone_angst_att_is_listening_on
    _twitter.php.

7. Alex Pentland researches, among other things, "reality mining": gleaning information from people's physical movements. Other researchers (Aguiton, Cardon, and Smoreda) talk about creating "live maps" of continually updated information, or speak of this area as "urban informatics" (Iveson). See "Rich Identity and the Next Net," October 2009, http://senseable.mit.edu/engagingdata /presentations/ED_Plenary_Pentland.pdf.

8. MIT SENSEable City Lab website, http://senseable.mit.edu.

9. Network & Society page, MIT SENSEable City Lab, http://senseable.mit.edu/network/.

10. Arik Hesseldahl, "There's Gold in 'Reality Mining'," *Businessweek*, March 24, 2008, 2, http://www.businessweek. com/technology/content/mar2008/tc20080323_387127 _page_2.htm.

11. Alex Pentland, "Reality Mining of Mobile Communications: Toward a New Deal on Data," in *The Global Information Technology Report 2008–2009: Mobility in a Networked World*, eds. Soumitra Dutta and Irene Mia, World Economic Forum, 77.

12. Ibid, 75.

13. Alex (Sandy) Pentland, David Lazer, Devon Brewer, Tracy Heibeck, "Using Reality Mining to Improve Public Health and Medicine," a white paper commissioned by the Robert Wood Johnson Foundation, February 2009, http://senseable.mit .edu/engagingdata/papers/ED_SI_Using_Reality_Mining.pdf.

14. See, for example, the entry "Homophily, Serendipity, Xenophilia," April 25, 2008, http://www.ethanzuckerman. com/blog/2008/04/25/homophily-serendipity-xenophilia/.

SEVEN

## LOOKING FOR A MEANINGFUL RELATIONSHIP
*Making Data Make Sense*

1.  Quoted in "Big Data Is Less About Size, And More
    About Freedom," Techcrunch.com, March 16, 2010,
    http://techcrunch.com/2010/03/16/big-data-freedom.
2.  Evelyn Edson, *The World Map 1300–1492: The Persistence of
    Tradition and Transformation* (Baltimore: Johns Hopkins
    University Press, 2007), 15.
3.  Ibid., 23.
4.  Ibid., 31
5.  Geoff McGhee, *Journalism in the Age of Data*.
    Stanford University, video report, 54:00, July 2010,
    http://datajournalism.stanford.edu/#.
6.  Ibid.
7.  "Spark 91," *Spark*, CBC Radio, November 15 and 17, 2009.
8.  Ibid.
9.  A project of IBM Research and the IBM Cognos software
    group. See http://www-958.ibm.com/software/data
    /cognos/manyeyes/.
10. "7 Essential Skills You Didn't Learn in College,"
    Wired.com, September 27, 2010, http://www.wired.com
    /magazine/2010/09/ff_wiredu/all/1.
11. Andy Alexander, "Data analysis and the future of journalism,"
    *Washington Post*, November 30, 2010, http://voices
    .washingtonpost.com/ombudsman-blog/2010/11
    /data_analysis_and_the_furture.html.

12. See, for example, Tavia Grant, "Census Day, 2011 – Dawn of a New Information-Gathering Era," *Globe and Mail*, May 10, 2011, http://www.theglobeandmail.com/news/politics /census-day-2011-dawn-of-a-new-information-gathering -era/article2016837/page1/.

13. Lawrence Lessig, "Against Transparency: The Perils of Openness in Government," *The New Republic*, October 9, 2009, http://www.tnr.com/article/books-and-arts/against-transparency.

14. Ibid.

15. "Mining Social Networks: Untangling the Social Web," Technology Quarterly Q3 2010, *The Economist*, September 2, 2010, http://www.economist.com/node/16910031?story _id=16910031&fsrc=rss.

16. Albert-László Barabási, *Bursts: The Hidden Pattern Behind Everything We Do* (New York: Dutton, 2010), 198–99.

EIGHT

**UNITE!**

*You Have Nothing to Lose But Your Terms-of-Service Contract!*

1. Ryan Singel, "Facebook's Gone Rogue; It's Time for an Open Alternative," Wired.com, May 7, 2010, http://www.wired.com /epicenter/2010/05/facebook-rogue/.

2. Jason Calacanis, "The Big Game, Zuckerberg and Overplaying Your Hand," Calacanis.com, May 12, 2010, http://calacanis.com /2010/05/12/the-big-game-zuckerberg -and-overplaying-your-hand/.

3. Michelle Madejski, Maritza Johnson, and Steven M. Bellovin, "The Failure of Online Social Network Privacy Settings," Technical Report CUCS-010-11, Department of Computer Science, Columbia University, February 2011, https://mice.cs.columbia.edu/getTechreport.php?techreportID=1459.

4. Elias Bizannes, "What You Need to Know About Data Portability," Mashable.com, August 12, 2010, http://mashable.com/2010/08/12/data-portability/.

5. Ibid.

6. Ryan Singel, "Netflix Spilled Your *Brokeback Mountain* Secret, Lawsuit Claims," Wired.com, December 7, 2009, http://www.wired.com/threatlevel/2009/12/netflix-privacy-lawsuit/.

7. Narayanan and Shmatikov, "Robust De-anonymization of Large Datasets (How to Break Anonymity of the Netflix Prize Dataset)," Arxiv.org, February 5, 2008, http://arxiv.org/PS_cache/cs/pdf/0610/0610105v2.pdf.

8. Arvind Narayanan and Vitaly Shmatikov, "De-anonymizing Social Networks," Arxiv.org, 2009, http://arxiv.org/PS_cache/arxiv/pdf/0903/0903.3276v1.pdf.

9. Ben Rooney, "Non-EU Websites Must Operate Under EU Privacy Laws," *Wall Street Journal*, March 16, 2011, http://blogs.wsj.com/tech-europe/2011/03/16/non-eu-websites-must-operate-under-eu-privacy-laws/?mod=google_news_blog.

10. Ibid.

11. Eagle, "Engineering a Common Good."

12. Pentland, "Reality Mining of Mobile Communications."

13. Ibid., 79.

14. "Depressed Woman Loses Benefits Over Facebook Photos," CBC.ca, November 21, 2009, http://www.cbc.ca/news/canada/montreal/story/2009/11/19/quebec-facebook-sick-leave-benefits.html.

15. "Insurers Test Data Profiles to Identify Risky Clients,"
    *Wall Street Journal*, November 19, 2010.
16. Daniel J. Solove, *The Future of Reputation: Gossip, Rumor, and Privacy
    on the Internet* (New Haven, CT: Yale University Press, 2007).
17. Simson Garfinkel, "A Cloud Over Ownership," *Technology
    Review* (September/October 2011).
18. Ibid.
19. Solove, *The Future of Reputation*, 79.


NINE

## THE DATA MAP AND YOUR FUTURE
*Becoming a Data Activist*

1. Eagle, "Engineering a Common Good," 160.
2. Taylor, *Sources of the Self*, 160.
3. Ibid., 159.
4. Ibid.
5. Such as has been articulated by Eagle, "Engineering a
   Common Good."
6. Greenfield is Founder and Managing Director of the urban-
   systems design practice, Urbanscale. From the full version
   of the interview for *Spark*, posted April 28, 2011.